THE SUBURBAN PROPHET:
LIGHT BEINGS AMONG US

by

Rev. Adriana Dominguez

1st Edition Printed June, 2017
Printed in the U.S.A.

Acknowledgements

Special thanks to my friends Amy Atkins, Kate Cuskelly Smith and my cousin Veronica Santiago for your input. Also, many thanks to my family for your patience and support. This book contains only true stories, however, certain names have been changed to protect individual identities. I forever hold immense appreciation for everyone who participated in these experiences.

Introduction

This is a book about the spiritual beings that live and walk among us and how you can partner with them to achieve an awesome life experience. I never thought a sentence like that would ever come out of my mouth. Even with all the mind-blowing things I have witnessed in my life. Even with all the evidence I've been given, there was still a part of me that resisted accepting what I'd always suspected was true. That is, until the evening of June 30, 2015.

Ever since I was a child I've had a strong desire, okay I've been obsessed, with uncovering the real meaning of life. I realize I'm admitting I wasn't a normal kid, but I had to know. What are we doing here? Why did we come? Were we sent for a reason? If so, what was it?

As a child, I can remember relentlessly questioning the leaders at our local church about why things were done the way they were. I wanted answers to certain rules, such as why we had to eat fish on Fridays. Why did women have to cover their heads when they entered church? I realize now that I was trying to make sense of what God wants from us. I was trying to understand God and God's reason for bringing us to earth in the first place. The answers I received from those in charge telling me, "Because that's just the way it's always been done," only served to frustrate and push me to look for better answers.

At a very young age, a deep knowing within me shouted that there was much more to this life than we can see and I desperately wanted to know what it was. I wondered if perhaps, like in the story of Adam and Eve, we did something wrong and were banished from heaven as a punishment. If it had been our own choice, why would we ever choose to come to a world where both good and bad things happen? If God loves us, why can't life always be good? And is God even a he?

The persistence of my desire to know must have caught the attention of the "universal powers that be," because I have received some awesome answers to my relentless questioning. It's been an incredible ride that I wouldn't have changed for anything. Okay, maybe a thing or two. But, overall, the things that have occurred in response to my unrelenting search for meaning have been more than amazing. Now that so much has been revealed to me, I feel compelled to share it with you, so that you too may find peace in the knowledge of why we're here and what this life is all about.

I believe I've now discovered why we came, why our soul decided to incarnate into a physical body for a short while on this planet called Earth. I have discovered why prayers are sometimes answered and sometimes not. I know how prayer works. I also now realize that we are always praying. Every thought, word and action is a prayer, nothing goes unrecorded or unheard. I also know we have much more power available to us than we realize and how, in a few easy steps, you can learn to use this power in your own life - just as it was intended.

The fact is we are held in the highest esteem by the Source of the Universe. This Source of All Life will bend over backwards for us. Why? Because It owes us It's very life. Yes, without us, the power we call God would not exist. In short, I've learned that WE are the ones who are adored and why. I have also discovered why we suffer and why we came into a world which allows it.

As these secrets are revealed to you, I have no doubt your heart and mind will soar with the knowledge that we humans are the most awesome and blessed beings that walk the face of this Universe. Come with me and discover who the team of beings are that signed up to make this journey with you and how partnering with them will turn your life into a magnificent adventure.

Chapter 1
Five Words

The crash of her keys as they landed on my desk shattered the silence in my office like breaking glass. Startled, I stared at them for a moment, sprawled out before me like a discarded rag doll. Before I had the chance to look up, I heard the impatient voice of my new boss. "Go move my car!" she demanded, turning on her heel and flying out of my office like a wicked whirling dervish. While I had been the recipient of some of her unreasonable directives, such as telling me who I could and could not spend my unpaid lunchtimes with, she typically saved the car relocation chore for her secretary. Poor Della received the brunt of her disrespect, handling it with more grace than I ever could. The mild mannered secretary would typically come in and find our boss's half eaten food plates sitting on her chair, forcing her to schlep them back to the employee cafeteria half a city block away before being able to start her days' work. Then, around 10:00 a.m. when her large Cadillac was about to be ticketed for being parked in a two-hour zone, our new boss would emerge from her office, bellowing at Della to perform her valet services. The two-hour zone was right outside the front door to our office, whereas the employee parking lot at our large hospital was at least a quarter mile away. So, it was a matter of convenience that fed our boss's need to wield disrespect over her staff. Whatever

1

the reason for her abuse, it did not sit well with me. I didn't like when she disrespected Della and, together with the unreasonable lunchtime directives, I definitely didn't like it when she did it to me.

Nevertheless, I arose from my desk and complied with her orders. Once in the car, I gunned the engine on that huge Cadillac, which forced it to lurch forward out of its parking slot like a scared jackrabbit. Task completed, I returned to my desk and started to remove my coat to get back to work. But, something stopped me. What was I doing, that "something" said? Sure, I'd been at this job for five years and I liked my work, but the environment over the past few months with this new boss had become absolutely unbearable. And it didn't show any signs of improving. Was I going to continue to allow myself to be abused? Well, was I? So, instead of taking off my coat, I picked up my purse and keys and walked out...forever.

I had just purchased my first home, a small townhouse yet a castle to me, only a couple months before. As a result, I had absolutely no money left in the bank. My dad had died a couple years prior, so I had no security person to fall back on in desperate moments like this. I had always feared being homeless and now my darkest fear had arrived at my door, pounding on it, demanding to be let in. Since that fear wasn't going away, I realized the only way around it was to look it in the face and push past. Typically overly responsible, I had never ever in my wildest dreams thought I'd ever walk off a

2

job. The anguish I now felt in my soul tore me apart. But, I am a survivor.

I have always known there was a forceful presence surrounding me - even when times got tough. I suppose I was in shock at having had the uncharacteristic nerve to do what I did. But, I believe that "Force" helped me go through the mindless motions of basic survival during those first few days of not knowing where my next meal was coming from. I made a doctor's appointment and was immediately put on stress-leave, which provided a thin, short-term shield between the homeless wolf at the door and myself. I made phone calls and sent out resumes. But the most significant thing I did, each and every day was to talk to that forceful presence. I didn't just talk to it, I implored it with every ounce of my being. I connected with it, as if the forceful presence was another person standing right in front of me.

For the next several weeks, I developed a routine. I would get up in the morning and talk to the Force. I knew they were listening. I don't know exactly why I felt that this Force was a "they," a gathering of souls if you will, versus one singular entity. But my overly-developed-since-childhood sixth-sense told me so. I believed I wasn't in that room alone. In fact, I absolutely knew my prayer was being heard. It wasn't an elaborate or ritualistic prayer, just a genuine outpouring of strong emotion coupled with mindful conviction.

With heartfelt passion flowing out of me like burning lava erupting out of a volcano, I repeated my simple, yet powerful feelings aloud. "I know you love me!" "I know you love me!" I cried. I offered this simple conviction to the spiritual team of beings who I knew surrounded me. I poured all the emotion and strength I possessed into that one phrase, over and over. The strong desire for a new job, the conviction that I was valuable and deserved to be cared for, the knowing I had done the right thing for my own self-respect, my fear of living on the street, the trust and conviction that I was not alone and was being heard. All those emotions and more went into that proclamation. Daily, I'd speak it strong, out loud, standing in the middle of my living room. Shaking and crying with a torrent of emotion. Not a cry of weakness, mind you, but one of strong conviction delivered with extreme intensity. Never did I blame anyone for my circumstances. I took complete responsibility for my decision, knowing I had done the right thing. I didn't waste or diffuse any of my energy in thinking or talking about how unreasonable my boss may have been. I focused only on what I wanted to have happen. Even though I was scared out of my mind, I held strong to my faith. I just knew this powerful spiritual force, which I would later come to understand is a team of beings imbued with the power of God, were with me throughout all this.

Each day I would spend several hours immersed in this powerful declaration offering with all the strength I possessed, the simple phrase, "I know you love me!" Then around 10 or 11 am, I would usually collapse onto the couch in an exhausted heap and fall asleep. The sound of the mailman at my door around 1:30 pm would typically wake me up. When I arose, my muscles would be sore from the intensity of clenching them while I'd been praying. However, never did I give into self-pity or defeatism. Failure was not an option and I knew it. I would then spend the rest of the afternoon sending out resumes and doing whatever needed to be done. When 5 o'clock rolled around, I would put everything away and focus on other things. Back in the early 90's when this occurred, offices were rarely opened past 5 pm, so I knew it was unlikely I'd be getting any phone calls for interviews. That's when I would rest and let it go. Until the next day, when I would repeat that daily ritual all over again.

Thankfully, my doctor had put me on "disability due to stress" which, because I had paid into it, allowed me to receive my full salary for up to 6 weeks. At week 5, he phoned me and said he could no longer sign for an extension on the claim, as I had reached the maximum allowable time limit. I thanked him for helping me and told him I understood, as the unmistakable scratching of the homeless wolf's claws grew louder at my door.

During this time I had been casually dating a gentleman named Dennis who worked at a company owned by Apple Computer. That Sunday as he was leaving my condo, he noticed a stack of resumes I was planning to mail out. He said, "Why don't you give me one of those and I'll see

5

if the VP of HR at my company knows of anyone who is looking for someone with your background." Since I had nothing to lose, I complied. I gave him exactly one resume.

Early the next morning, I received a call from the VP of HR who said he had run into Dennis in the executive restroom...yes, apparently that really happens. Dennis had told him about me and given him my resume. It just so happened that the VP was looking for someone with my *exact* skills and experience. It seemed their company had just received notice of an EEOC audit, for which my background was a perfect fit! I was hired as a temporary contractor on the spot and began work on the same Monday my disability insurance payments ran out – for one and a half times my previous salary. I might also add, this was the best environment I had ever worked in. The management team was extremely respectful of their employees and for one of the few times in my career, I felt valued. A three month contract turned into nine months, at which point I was able to obtain a management position in another well-known high tech firm, just as I had previously been looking for.

Amazing? Yes! Although I wasn't specifically aware of the particulars of how the Divine Force manifests itself in our lives, I just KNEW that something or someone up there loved me. Without realizing it, I had unwittingly tapped into the process which allows a direct exchange of energy between dimensions. That is, between our physical dimension and the non-physical spiritual dimension. The focus, fervor and conviction with which I offered my prayer during those tenuous weeks literally created a hole in the veil between two worlds, ours and that of Spirit. This allowed for the easy exchange of energy between our dimension and theirs. My incredible desire, coupled with a huge amount of trust sent a clear message to my Spiritual Support Team. It sent the message that my intention was not just to survive this situation, but to emerge from it a winner! You see, as I prayed my simple five word prayer each day with so much intensity, they went to work in the non-physical to gather other beings who could provide additional assistance. The longer I prayed, the more beings gathered. Consequently, more energy flowed towards rectifying my situation and moving that huge mountain.

Additionally, the fact that I would fall into an exhausted lump and sleep each day after these intense summoning sessions, allowed them to have me out of the way (along with any fear or worrying I might have done, which would have gotten in the way of their efforts). I have no doubt they gathered in my living room while I slept to discuss and strategize solutions.

It is imperative that after we express our desires, we get out of the way and let our spiritual team members do their work. It's like when you're not feeling well and someone offers to make a meal for you in your kitchen, but you keep checking up on them, interrupting their ability to effectively do their job. Getting out of the way, means putting our attention completely

7

elsewhere for a while. That gives our spiritual team the time and space they need to call in other beings for assistance who possess expertise in the area needing attention. These additional guardian angels, can then affect situations and behaviors of their own human charges on earth who can help us. Remember, everyone has a team and they all interact. It's an awesome thing to witness the power of the coming together of those who are able to create incredible outcomes.

There are several other important elements which must be understood in order to encourage the successful coming together of this "energy" which creates miracles. They are key in understanding how energy is exchanged between dimensions. And, they explain why prayers are not always answered. Once you learn how to relate to your team so they are more engaged in your daily life, you will be able to draw forth their assistance more easily. As you read on you will come to understand the elements necessary to create an environment within and around you which encourages a greater level of spiritual assistance.

The great lengths our team can go through to affect and orchestrate incredible results never fails to amaze me. Their capabilities are not fettered by time nor form, as they are not bound by physical laws. I consider them to be "aspects of the Divine." They are God's representatives, possessing spiritual powers which provide us support and assistance when needed. And, I believe we all – I repeat, WE ALL - have the ability to access assistance from these powerful entities who constantly walk beside us. All they need is our focus, our trust, our communication and our desire for an on-going partnership. I say partnership, because that assumes a relationship and adds the element of co-creativity. Consider yourself as the driver of the ship, while your spiritual team is the engine. Working together to create a divine life experience is how it is done. One element requires the other.

The power of your attention is very strong, it equals the power of your intention. Your intention draws to you energies in the form of spiritual light beings who begin to gather as soon as you have declared it. It's like they get the clear message, "Okay, we're going this way now." The longer you hold your intention, the more it creates a feeling of conviction. Your conviction acts like a beacon attracting even more spiritual beings who share and support your same conviction. Their energy creates a force that shares your same understanding, "We're headed in this direction and this is the way it is going to be when we get there." If you have heard of The Law of Attraction, it basically states, "That which is like itself is drawn." If you are confused or distracted, your energy is also diffused, so you will not be able to attract much assistance. If you are focusing your energy into feelings of hopelessness and powerlessness, that is what you will attract. No one who is powerful wants to hang around to hear about what can't be done and why, not even the most compassionate angelic being. Your spiritual support team members hear what you say, not just through your words, but through your thoughts, feelings and convictions. The energy of those feelings and convictions either enhances or dulls your spiritual team's ability to perform miracles in your life. If you are emanating negativity, you will be surrounded by energies that are negative or defeatist in nature, they will block you from being able to receive the powerful positive creative assistance which is available to you. Conversely, if you are emanating a strong positive conviction, telling yourself and all that surrounds you that your intent is to emerge a winner in this situation, that is the energy of the forces who will be drawn to you.

If I had spent a lot of time in anger over what had happened with my job, assigning blame and re-hashing details about that which I could no longer control, the focus of my energy would have changed. Similarly, if I had focused my energy solely on the fear I was feeling, <u>or anything other than the outcome I was expecting</u>, my experience would have been much different. It would have weakened my intention to receive assistance. I believe our spiritual team members thrive on our courage, our strength and our steadfast conviction. It sends a very clear message and makes it easier for them to use that energy to fuel their own power and enthusiasm.

Their love for us is immense. Our spiritual support team shares in our earthly life experience to the degree of our sustained invitation. This is one of the keys. Our awareness of their presence, our welcoming of their support and our return of their appreciation creates a circle that allows the flow of the greatest power in the universe, love. You may not win the lotto, but your entire life - even the challenging parts - will become much more remarkable than you ever dreamed possible.

Chapter 2
The Clipping

When I was about 4 years old, I remember walking past a lovely bed of roses my dad had planted next to the garage on the side of our house. As the early morning dew glistened like diamonds on their velvet petals, I could actually feel love and admiration coming from those roses! Time seemed to stand still as the dawn mist rolled in and lent a soft focus to the entire scene in front of me. As I gazed into their beautiful faces, I realized those roses were alive. I remember feeling a powerful surge of appreciation course through me, go straight into them and be immediately returned in kind. It wasn't until years later that I discovered there is indeed a very real connection between all living things, which can be measured electronically. But back then, I only knew I could feel their magic. And that's when the Universe, like the rose, decided to offer up some of its secrets. It must have accurately concluded those secrets would not be lost on me, since I was definitely paying attention.

It was around this time that I started having many paranormal experiences. I would often envision or receive a thought that I knew came from a source other than my own. For the most part, I would share it with my parents, but not always.

When I was about 5 years old, I remember describing some people who were coming to visit us who were acquaintances of my parents, but who I had never met myself. I told my mother they would be arriving in a blue car with a strange "thing" around the steering wheel. My mother corrected me saying, "No. Their car isn't blue, it's brown." When the visitors arrived, it was in their newly painted car, having been changed from brown to baby blue just two days prior. As they walked us around it, they proudly showed off a leather steering wheel cover they had just purchased to go with the car's new paint job. They said they had just picked up the car that afternoon, having had to wait for it an extra day due to rain. Our house was the first stop they had made in their new blue car.

On another occasion around age 7, I described in great detail, a mean spirited woman who I had also never met before. My mother and I were going to her home to inquire about renting it. On the way there, I explained to my mother that the woman would be sitting on the front porch when we arrived. I said she would be wearing a flowered dress with red buttons on it and that she would be "very mean." Unfortunately, everything I said was true.

There were several other occurrences like this when I was a child. The last of this specific type happened when I was about 12. I was riding in the backseat of our family car and my parents were seated in front. We were driving down the freeway as I said, "There is going to be an accident." My father, who believed in me (except apparently not on that day) uttered, "Oh, you're crazy!" I went ahead and buckled my seatbelt anyway, but being a very sensitive child, his words had stung me.

About a quarter of a mile further down the road we exited the freeway. At the end of the off-ramp, we came to stop. Almost immediately after we stopped, two cars hit head-on right in front of us. Fortunately, nobody was seriously hurt in that accident, as one car was stopped at the time and the other wasn't going very fast. A young man immediately got out of one car and spit blood out onto the pavement. The light turned green for us and my dad drove on. Both my parents remained in complete silence. I took that to mean that they did indeed believe I was crazy. As a result, I didn't have any further premonitions of that type for a very long time.

A few years ago, following my dad's death, I found a newspaper clipping buried among his belongings. Apparently, my dad didn't think I was so crazy after all. In fact, because he took the time to submit my story to Bill Fiset's column in the Oakland Tribune a few months following the incident, I think he was rather proud of my gift.

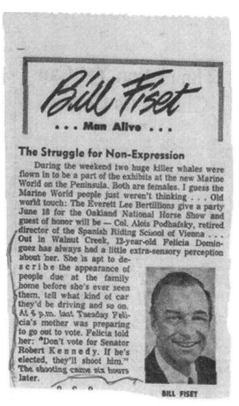

Bill Fiset

... Man Alive ...

The Struggle for Non-Expression

During the weekend two huge killer whales were flown in to be a part of the exhibits at the new Marine World on the Peninsula. Both are females. I guess the Marine World people just weren't thinking . . . Old world touch: The Everett Lee Bertillions give a party June 18 for the Oakland National Horse Show and guest of honor will be — Col. Alois Podhajsky, retired director of the Spanish Riding School of Vienna . . . Out in Walnut Creek, 12-year-old Felicia Dominguez has always had a little extra-sensory perception about her. She is apt to describe the appearance of people due at the family home before she's ever seen them, tell what kind of car they'd be driving and so on. At 6 p.m. last Tuesday Felicia's mother was preparing to go out to vote. Felicia told her: "Don't vote for Senator Robert Kennedy. If he's elected, they'll shoot him." The shooting came six hours later.

BILL FISET

(Note: Felicia is my middle name. Which, for some reason, my parents always preferred.)

I am very thankful to my dad for having saved that newspaper clipping, because it serves as proof of the fact that I was blessed - in case I'm ever tempted to forget. It also serves as proof of his love and respect for me, for which I am extremely grateful.

Because I was a very loving child (remember my exchange with the roses) and also incredibly sensitive (I cried for days when my dad mistakenly threw out my old doll, Somba) I believe I was born with what is known in the spiritual

16

world as a high vibration. A person's "vibration" is the term that describes the degree to which they are conscious of and allow the Source of All Life to flow through them. This Source is immense love coupled with the power behind life itself. You could refer to it as the power of love, because love drives and sustains it. The more you allow this life force to flow through and around you, the higher and stronger your vibration. The stronger your vibration, the greater beacon you are to attracting attention from all the powerful beings which this Source, or God, has imbued as God's divine representatives. These beings are able to channel the power of the Source and, therefore, have the ability to create what, from our perspective, appear to be miracles. For them, however, it's all in a day's work.

Now granted, my extremely sensitive nature has allowed me to become aware of things in my environment which some people might miss or take for granted. However, I believe intuition and the ability to attract miracles are abilities you, too, can develop with practice and dedication. I cannot emphasize this enough. EVERYONE has the capability to develop a personal relationship with their spiritual team. This relationship, in turn, will hone your intuitive skills and create within you the ability to attract awesome miracles into your life. The key is to expand your understanding of a few things in order to embrace new paradigms that will pull miracles into your life like magicians pull rabbits out of hats.

The first thing we need to expand is our understanding of the power we call God. Contrary to popular belief, God is NOT an old man sitting on a cloud. God is not anything separate from us. We are all part of this immense power which creates worlds. There is no separation. That power did, after all, create us. Therefore, the DNA of the Divine Source Itself flows through our very veins. We are, each of us, an integral part of this Life Force. Without us the puzzle of life itself would not be complete. For too long we have been taught that God is something akin to an old man who sits in a far-away heaven, arbitrarily raining down blessings and misfortunes, who is unpredictable and often hard to please. That concept of God made in man's image was developed by people in power in order to control the masses of humanity through fear.

The truth is that we are all part of the immensely powerful Divine Source of Life, and as such we have the right and *responsibility* to claim that power. In doing so, we draw to ourselves an awesome life experience right here and now, even in the context of our current life circumstances. However, you must be willing to start from where you are by beginning to notice the small miracles that come your way every day. In doing so, you automatically begin to draw to yourself energies that will help you in attracting more supernatural phenomenons, both large and small. Shortly, I will demonstrate how this works on a practical level.

No matter the state of development of your own vibration, I believe everyone possesses this capability. That is, the ability to connect to and receive incredible assistance from God, the Source of All Life, *as well as the team* of powerful non-physical beings who surrounds each of us. This collective group is our Spiritual Support Team ("SST" for short). We each have a group of these beings who volunteered to stick with us through the good, bad and the ugly and provide us with support throughout this life. The only caveat is that we must engage them. As previously stated, I have come to understand that they are individuated aspects of the Divine. Similar to facets on a diamond, they are able to focus the powerful light energy from the Source into specific areas of our lives. They are similar to us, but without the limitation our finite physical forms and perspectives place on us. As we progress through this book, you will receive evidentiary proof that this team is very real and available to you to the degree of your sustained intention on achieving a connection with them.

For now, I want you to hold in your heart the truth that without you the Universal Source of Life would not exist in the completeness that it does. For you are and always will be an important part of It. Now is the time to embrace your true nature as an incredibly valuable and awesomely loved part of this system - that is, the system of life itself. Don't look for evidence of mediocrity, rather begin to see the truth. That you are imbued with and surrounded by an incredible power that flows in, around and through you. If you allow it and call it forth with faith, this power can and will work through you to deliver an enriched life experience.

As a simple example of this presence, one day I decided to visit my favorite craft store and was disappointed to find that I had forgotten my coveted discount coupons. This store regularly mails out coupons that offer a significant savings and I always try to remember to take mine with me when I go. As I entered the checkout line with my items, I looked around and noticed everyone clutching their precious coupons like little kids with their milk money. Again, I felt some annoyance at not having remembered to bring my own. As the line moved forward I felt something tugging at my feet and realized some pieces of paper were sticking to my shoes. Annoyed, I tried to kick them away as the line inched forward, but they seemed to follow me. I finally bent down to remove the bothersome obstruction. There between my feet were not just one, but several coupons. I looked around, but everyone seemed to have theirs. The lady behind me said, "They must have been put there for you." I smiled and suddenly realized she was right! Because of my annoyance, I had almost missed a sweet gift. You might say that this was insignificant. You might think that things like this happen every day and you would be right. Things like this do happen every day. I've come to realize that as we notice and appreciate the abundance of small miracles that come our way each and every day, while acknowledging their true source, we begin to

20

attract bigger ones. That day at the craft store I realized there was something else at work in our lives on a daily basis than just mere coincidence.

Although I've caught a lot of them, I can't help but wonder how many other blessings I've missed. I'd be willing to bet miracles, both large and small, show up in your life all the time as well. Miracles that you could be missing. When we do catch them, we often tend to write them off as luck or coincidence. In today's fast-paced world we are so preoccupied with what's coming up next, that we often forget to cultivate an awareness of the moment. The more you work on noticing the small incidents of divine gifts that come your way, the more appreciation you'll feel. Appreciation is a strong vibration, because it is similar to love. Both send strong signals to your Spiritual Support Team saying, "I'm in receptive mode. Send me more of this, please." In this mode you become a magnet, pulling to yourself more assistance from your team. And, once you've got the attention of one of them, more will gather. That is because, like the rose, they offer appreciation to you in response to your vibrational offering of appreciation to them. As they themselves offer the vibration of appreciation, more light beings are attracted to them and so on. This is because you become more fun to be around. You create a "party" of beings who are drawn to appreciation. These are beings who operate on love and they are the ones you want around you.

21

I was recently reading an on-line posting from a young man who had slept through his alarm clock then heard a voice distinctly say his name. It was loud enough to wake him up, which in turn kept him from being late for work. Although the voice was distinctly audible, he wrote it off as a dream. A few weeks later, it happened again. It was the same voice. This time he bolted and sat straight up in bed. In his post, he was asking people what they thought. Below his post were several responses, most saying it was all in his mind. Following those was a response from a person who immediately condemned him, saying he should "question his own arrogance, because no one is above anyone else." This person's comment likely stemmed from his own feeling of unworthiness and jealousy. However, it reflects what many believe about miracles - that they are available only to saints and biblical characters, not to ordinary people like you and me. It is no surprise then that the multitude of miracles we experience every day, starting with the fact that our hearts continue to beat on their own until the day we die, often go completely unnoticed and unappreciated by us.

We need to remember that we are spiritual beings merely having a temporary physical experience. We are spiritual beings, first and foremost, which makes us part of the Godhead. We are not lowly or unworthy. Quite to the contrary. We came here to do incredibly important work. The work we do actually allows the universe to remain sustainable.

Our presence here gives us an enhanced opportunity to appreciate our own immense and unique capabilities. These capabilities include, but are not limited to trust, courage, faith and strength. In heaven we don't have opportunities to experience the challenges that are available here on earth, so we don't get to practice our own capabilities. This is one of the reasons we chose to come here. In case you were wondering, that is a huge gift. This earth, with everything from beauty and love to hate and corruption is the best place in creation to see, feel and love ourselves as the incredibly capable beings we truly are!

Because we had the courage to come to earth, our spiritual team members also get to share in these special opportunities. One is to generate true compassion, and compassion is the heart of love. This is an opportunity for which they are immensely grateful. They also get to appreciate their own capabilities in shining the light of God through themselves into our earthly life experience.

It is, therefore, through our experiences here that the power of love, which is the Source of all Creation, continues and grows. The more we appreciate the significant role we play in the continuance of life itself, the more readily we can accept our honored place among the chosen. So, if you're ever prone to feeling small and insignificant, stop. You are indeed an anointed one. You are not just worthy, but you are one of the reasons the heavens sing. Your Spiritual Support Team's gratitude towards you is immense and they love to express their appreciation. You are such a significant piece of the tapestry of creation, your very existence enriches the life of God.

Somba and me

Chapter 3
The Team

When I was in the first grade, we moved to another town and I was attending a new school. My mother and I moved into my aunt Mary's small 3 bedroom home in Hayward. This was a temporary move while we waited for a new house to be built. However, telling a child something is temporary makes little to no difference, as at that age, the present moment is all there is. Needless to say, I was feeling a bit stressed by my change in environment, but I was doing my best to adjust to my new surroundings. Out on the playground one day, I happened to look up. There up over the roof of the small building that housed the bathrooms at Sequoia Elementary School I "saw" an opaque vision of three people sitting behind what appeared to be a desk. The vision was somewhat hazy, but I realized that one of the beings resembled my aunt Mary. These three beings appeared to be watching me on some type of monitor that was sitting on a desk facing them. To me this monitor looked like a TV set. The three of them sat peering into it intently and, somehow, I knew they were observing me through it.

Now, remember that when I was in the first grade in 1964, the personal computer was far from being invented. I had this vision more than once while out there on that playground. I just assumed that my auntie must be wanting to keep tabs on me while I was at school. I called the box they were looking into a "register." I'm not sure where that word came from, but it was the word that popped into my mind. Sometimes when I'd get home I'd almost be tempted to ask my aunt if she'd seen me out on that playground that day using her register. However, like many of the things I experienced when I was little, I realized they were other-worldly in nature and made the wise decision to keep what I'd seen to myself.

So, how could aunt Mary be watching me while she was at home several blocks away? Well, my aunt had always loved me and I her. To this day I believe my beloved aunt Mary who now resides in heaven, is part of the group of souls who remains available to me. I believe the group of beings I saw above the bathrooms that day included the part of her soul which remained in heaven while she was on earth. This phenomenon is described very well in the book, The Afterlife of Billy Fingers. Through his sister, Billy does a great job of communicating his experiences after he died suddenly. He explains that part of our soul remains on the other side and never completely incarnates on earth. Yes, our soul is that huge. Because my aunt Mary is part of my spiritual support team, it makes complete sense that she was one of the beings in the group I could see watching me out on the playground. And because of some unusual things that occurred following her death several years later, I assume that is the case. Ultimately, my beloved and awesome aunt

Mary helped me prove a theory from beyond her grave. And, since I've now performed the same experiment several times, I am convinced it works.

After I had my children, my family and I moved to a new area and shortly discovered we weren't real happy there for several reasons. My aunt Mary had recently died and I decided to try an experiment. I asked her to intercede for us with the powers that be, because we needed help. Although I was anxious and a bit upset about our situation, I worked very hard to relax about it and I did everything I could to help myself feel better. As we've already discussed, asking then relaxing and letting it go, are key to becoming more "attractive" to your spiritual team. This is because extreme stress makes it hard for them to pick up our intention. It is also important that you continue to move in a direction which demonstrates your respect for yourself by doing things that help you feel better. This sends a clear message that your intention in this situation is to emerge a winner, that you are a spiritual warrior and will not allow yourself to be defeated by anything or anybody. You are in effect holding open the "winner" door as you anticipate assistance in achieving your desired outcome. We did not come forth to anticipate defeat nor to be complacent. We are spiritual warriors and although sensitivity is a virtue, weakness is not okay under any circumstance. Angels carry swords for a reason and losing is not one of them.

27

It is obvious when you're receiving supernatural assistance, because things often happen very quickly and fall into place supernaturally. There is a lot of synchronicity involved. Timing is everything and the eloquence with which our SST engineers and directs certain players and situations never ceases to amaze me. Within a month of my request, we ended up with a new home that coincidentally resembled my aunt's old house back in Hayward - although this one was a complete remodel of two duplexes having been stripped down to the studs and remade into one large home.

We were able to sell the house we were living in without having to pay a sales commission - which we couldn't afford anyway. We had found out that the house across the street was (coincidentally) going on the market and an open house was going to be held the next day. So, we bought a few balloons and a "For Sale" sign and put it out on our own lawn. People coming to view the house across the street started coming over to see ours as well. And voila - within a few hours it sold to a loan agent who even ended up completing all the paperwork for us!

At this same time a realtor we had met showed us a house he had heard was coming on the market, but didn't have a listing on yet. He said "I don't know why I'm showing this to you, since I don't have a listing on it yet and can't sell it, but I just want you to see what's out there." When we were viewing the home, the gardener smiled and said hello to me in Spanish. Something about him seemed familiar to me, so I went up to talk to him about the landscaping work he was doing on the property. I remember asking him a question about the cost of the home that he couldn't answer. He said I should call the owner for that information and gave me the phone number.

From that moment on everything seemed to move in surreal motion, but very quickly. The bottom line is that house was ours within a few weeks and we were able to move in the same day we moved out of our old house. Even though I was under no obligation to, I went ahead and paid the realtor who "didn't know why he was showing us the house," a considerable cash bonus, because I felt it was only fair. He was not very appreciative of what I had done, but there was no way to explain to him that it wasn't me...it was the other-worldly power around me that I'd tapped into. The power that can make magic happen.

The success of this situation proved the theory I held at the time that when our loved ones pass they remain available to us and are incredibly tuned in to our needs. My theory was that especially during the 2-4 month period following their deaths, we have easy access to their help. They wish to do everything they can for the ancestors they leave behind while they still have strong ties to and fresh memories of the physical world. Since then I have learned that they remain available to us throughout our lifetimes. A strong sustained focus on them invokes their assistance. This is why lighting candles in Hispanic homes on altars is known to be a powerful practice. The flame of the candle is a live reminder and simultaneous "invoker" of the presence of a spiritual entity. It lets them know we are thinking of them and that they are welcome, encouraged and invited to share in our daily life.

My aunt Mary had purchased several homes in her lifetime, so she had a particular affinity for real estate. She also had a very soft spot in her heart for children, having raised not just her own, but several extended family member's kids as well. My family was wanting to make this move in order for our children to live in a better environment. All these facts made my loving aunt Mary the perfect being to request assistance from. I'm very appreciative to her for not just helping us find a new home, but for helping me prove my theory.

Although I've had many signs of the presence of the loving beings who surround us, it wasn't until I read a book written by Natalie Sudman, that I was introduced to the fact that a spiritual group who works on our behalf really exists. After reading Natalie's account of meeting her own spiritual team during her near-death experience in Iraq, I began to investigate further. What my own investigations revealed from researching many other near death experiences (when people have died for a period of time and then returned to tell their stories) is that we each have a large group of powerful beings who *volunteered* to accompany us throughout our earth life. These beings are committed to remaining with us during this lifetime from start to finish. They are quite real and possess incredible super-natural capabilities. This is because they are Light Bearers who can deliver the powers of God through focused energy channels, similar to the way prisms focus and direct sunlight. They also have an enhanced vision of what's going on around us from their higher perspective. Unfettered by time they can easily look into the future and past to strategize moves like skilled chess players. Free from the limitations of form, they can literally move mountains to achieve certain outcomes.

I am not sure why most religions have not promoted the existence of such awesome spiritual beings who are available to us. Unless, perhaps, it has not been revealed to the irrefutable degree to those in charge of these organizations as it has to me and a few others. It is also possible that fear, disbelief and ridicule have kept those who have had such direct experiences from coming forth. Whatever the case, I strongly believe that if the existence of our spiritual support teams had been revealed to us sooner, life on this planet would be much richer. Our lives would be more meaningful and our world would be a much happier and kinder place. People would never, ever, feel alone, unsupported or hopeless again.

In her book entitled "Application of Impossible Things," Natalie Sudman meticulously chronicled her near death experience after being blown up by a roadside bomb while working for the Army as a civilian in Iraq. During her journey

31

to the other side, or into what she calls "Expanded Consciousness," she visited several levels of spiritual realms. She referred to the final place she visited on the other side before returning to her body here on earth as the "Jumping Off Place." As she described it, I envisioned a scene similar to a first time skydiver's. Picture the airplane door open while several experienced jumpers are issuing you your final instructions. You hang onto their every word, because you know your successful mission depends on following their input. Following are her words of what happened right before she returned to her body.

Nine personalities are with me in this environment, she writes. *All nine are intimately familiar. Some people or ideologies might refer to these personalities as guides, and some might perceive them as guardian angels. My own perception is that they are friendly and adept personalities who voluntarily fill a particular role that includes guidance, protection, and assistance. They maintain a broad focus and offer a "touchpoint" for me while I maintain the intense focus necessary to function effectively within physical existence.*

Their skills are equal to mine while their viewpoint from outside physical reality allows them to assist me in ways that would be particularly difficult to replicate were we all working from within the physical realm. These personalities are able to project trajectories and thereby assist me with avoiding unexpected clashes, physical threats, or side-

tracking off the broad course of interest intended by the Whole Self. I think of them now similarly to the way I thought of my personal security detail (PSD) in Iraq: my energy-level PSD team. In Iraq we were accompanied by an armed PSD guard team whenever we traveled off the base. They gathered intelligence prior to travel, planned routes, drove the armored vehicles, and guarded us while we inspected construction sites. My energy PSD team maintains a broad view of interactions, scopes out and advises my subconscious or unconscious toward productive routes, and guards me against unexpected intersections of experience. In addition to PSD-type duties, these personalities offer advice, run energy errands, and offer support, ultimately at my own direction and request. As equals, they are friends and colleagues, similar to friends and colleagues on the physical plane who help us think through decisions, offer a perspective we might miss, and watch our backs when we need that. They are full support without being directors. If I were to say, "Don't help with this – I want to do that on my own, even if it takes me a long time to figure out within the physical environment," then they would stand back and watch (probably falling all over themselves laughing. They seem to have a tendency for fond humor that is only really funny when firmly fixed in an expanded consciousness perspective. This can be a little irritating…).

Although in this scene we don't affect the physical environment in any way, these personalities have the capacity

33

to affect the physical in many ways. Appearing to have few limitations, they can influence thought patterns, create situations or coordinate entire events, enter dreams, temporarily take on a body, or communicate with me through an audible voice or visual flashes. They are able to manipulate physical energies in ways that would be perceived by us as moving solid objects or even creating them.

Reading this account of the actual interaction with her team (and subsequently, others who had also "died" and came back to tell their stories) cemented what I had previously suspected. That we are all, indeed, surrounded by a group of spiritual beings who made a commitment to remain with us throughout our lifetime on earth.

Natalie goes on to share a story of how her spiritual team interceded and calamity was once avoided when she was out walking her dog. She made it clear that intercession, while not consciously invoked, occurred as the calamity would have "served no purpose."

One such intervention occurred for me when I was driving on a narrow two-lane road as a teenager. My friend and I were talking and not paying particular attention. We were going the speed limit, which was 55 mph and there was a large van driving ahead of us. I could not see around the van and I had only left one or two car lengths between us. We were traveling along at a pretty good clip when all of a sudden the horn on my car blasted. At the exact moment this occurred and I was shocked awake, the van in front of me swerved around a car that was completely stopped in the middle of the road making a left turn. I was able to quickly swerve onto the right shoulder, bottoming out my car in a pothole and then veered back onto the roadway. I was in complete shock, but safe. Had my horn not gone off seemingly by itself, I would have hit the stationary car in front of us, likely killing myself and others.

Obviously, not all communications are as strong as the one I received that day on the two-lane highway. However, I have found that the more energy I focus into developing and maintaining a relationship with my spiritual team members, the more benefit I experience from their presence. That is because they are also benefiting from our relationship. It is a give and take thing.

The relationship with our spiritual support team members is like any other one. The more effort we put into it, the stronger that relationship becomes. The more time and energy you put into building a true friendship with your team members, the more time and energy they will dedicate towards you. That is not because they are seeking praise in order to send you goodies, it is simply a natural thing. The more effort you put into creating a connection with anyone who is sincerely interested in creating a relationship with you, the more they will focus their attention on you. This is also the way the universe works at a quantum physics level. Like energy attracts like energy.

Cleve Backster was a brilliant man who performed thousands of experiments on how various life forms communicate with one another. He was able to measure their reactions to people around them. Some of his incredible experiments can be seen on youtube and on my website, www.revadriana.com. These experiments demonstrate the inner-connectivity and natural communication system which exists between all life forms. The first time Mr. Backster reported having this experience was on February 2, 1966 when he was up late working on some experiments using a polygraph machine. The polygraph machine measures physiological indices on humans such as blood pressure, pulse, respiration, and skin conductivity while the subject is asked a series of questions. It is also capable of measuring subtle physiological changes in other life forms when presented with a stimulus in their environment. This evening, he decided to hook it up to the leaf of a large Philodendron plant in his office. A normal back and forth reading was soon established by the needle, as the machine recorded its physiological output. He decided to water the plant and see if he could get a reaction from it. Upon doing so, he noticed a jump in the needle, but nothing significant. He then wondered what would happen if he decided to harm the plant by burning it. Since he had no matches handy, he rose from his chair and went into his secretary's office to retrieve her cigarette lighter (this was in 1966 when people smoked at work). As soon as he returned, he discovered something astonishing had occurred. Examining the print-out, he realized that at the exact moment he decided to harm the plant by burning the leaf, the needle attached to the plant had gone wild. The plant had telepathically received his intent to harm it and had experienced a surge of fear. He said from that moment on, his view of how everything in life is connected completely changed.

There is also a scene in the movie, "I Am" where producer/director Tom Shaydak visits the Heart Math organization in Northern California. Heart Math is one of several organizations which use electronic probes, similar to the polygraph, to measure the effect of our emotion backed thoughts on the world around us. As Tom sits in front of a plate of yogurt, which contains live acidophilus cultures, the yogurt is hooked up via probes to the monitoring device which measures its response to stimuli. There is not much measurable response until Tom is asked "Are you married?" As Tom thinks about his ex-wife, which elicits strong emotions from him, the needle measuring the live acidophilus culture immediately swings wildly. Again, when he is asked about his agent and then his lawyer, who he's been involved in challenges with, both thoughts elicit strong emotions from him which are immediately felt and experienced by the live yogurt culture. Note that the live culture was not attached to Tom in any way. Only the probes were attached to the yogurt to measure its response. Tom had nothing attached to him. He was merely sitting in the same room. The acidophilus culture is a microscopic life form that is not visible to the naked eye, yet it was able to sense and experience the emotion Tom was eliciting.

These experiments prove that the universe is engineered so that everything around you knows and responds to the feelings you emanate. The degree of response by the life forms around us directly correlates to the intensity of the emotions we express. This is very important in understanding how our Spiritual Support Team receives and returns our non-verbal information. The greater emotion we put into our communications with them, the easier they can hear us and the stronger their response will be. Emotion can be a simple as your focus on them. That is because your focus inherently carries a large degree of appreciation. And, as you already know, appreciation is a vibration that is very similar to love.

Mr. Backster's numerous experiments led him to conclude that, "Human thought backed with a little emotion, can be a very powerful thing." Indeed, our thoughts backed with emotions such as appreciation, anticipation and determination, literally serve as magnets to our beloved Spiritual Team members. They, are then compelled to return similar energy to us, just like the rose was drawn to return my shower of appreciation. I could feel it's appreciation in my heart, just like I can feel my team members' presence. I have practiced it so much now, that when I concentrate, I can feel them in the room just like I can another person. And, If I had ten-thousand tongues, I could never begin to thank them enough for their presence and involvement in my daily life.

So what is it that cares so deeply about us that it wants to know our every thought, feeling and impulse? What is it that is so interested in us? It is the very essence of the Life Force Itself, that's what. And yes, you are that significant a part of it.

When you become aware of your team members and invite them to communicate with you, the information and assistance you receive will be much clearer for you to "hear." It comes in the form of a feeling, which can be either subtle or intense. Or a thought whispered into your mind, or a phrase that seems uttered into your ear which does not come from any conscious thought you've generated. Signs appear everywhere, people who can help you appear out of nowhere. Situations occur that can lead to incredible opportunities, which of course, are up to you to follow. You will even begin to notice how your gaze is automatically shifted to something you need to be aware of at just the right moment. These things occur because, like the exchange of love between the rose and me, when you make the decision to have a real relationship with your team, they are drawn to support you in significant ways. You are simultaneously a beacon and a magnet, as you open yourself to their guidance.

Just like your physical friends who enjoy sharing your life, your Spiritual Team members who are in harmony with your intentions, will naturally be drawn to you. However, since they have been anointed by the Power of God, their abilities far exceed any possessed by your physical friends. That said, it is important to remember that we do not worship them, but rather we partner with them in order to enjoy an enriched life here on earth. They are spiritual beings with the Light of God focusing through them. Our focus on them, in turn, gives them the opportunity to experience moments of this life right alongside of us.

They have just asked me to clarify that it is a "symbiotic relationship" and one best enjoyed solely due to the opportunity for mutual enjoyment versus any particular agenda on either part. In other words, we mustn't think we are going to get everything we want just by becoming friends with them. That cannot and will not happen for a variety of reasons, our personal growth being the main agenda we share. Any healthy relationship is based on mutual give and take. What we provide for them is the opportunity for expansion from a distance. What they give us is love, support and the benefit of their larger view from a much higher perspective - 24/7. So, whatever your life experience, make sure it is an enriching one, for both sides. And remember it is our focus on trusting them to be with us which draws them close.

Chapter 4
A Rock

Inviting a two-way communication with your Spiritual Support Team is the best way to encourage that relationship. The way to accomplish this is personal to everyone. However, it is very important that you encourage your team to interact with you on a regular basis by learning how to effectively communicate with them. Developing this practice makes it easier to receive information and assistance. I typically start each morning by inviting my team in to share my day. As soon as I awaken, I send myself a huge mental hug and feelings of appreciation. Then, before any other thought about the world can seep in, I acknowledge and thank my team members for their presence and look for things to be grateful for. Because even on bad days, there is always something to be grateful for. And, just like our physical friends, our SST is attracted by our sense of appreciation and gratitude. However, it's just as important to remember that they are with us in times of sadness, frustration or fear as well. But, a grateful heart works wonders at lifting any emotional heaviness, making it easier for *us* to feel *their* presence and to remember we are not alone in whatever we might be going through.

Throughout my day, I routinely involve them in my activities - even the simple or mundane ones. For example, I never drive off in my car without invoking the presence of Jesus and Arc Angel Michael, both powerful protectors. In times of illness, I frequently call on Arc Angel Raphael the great healer, as well as my young cousin Branden, a young family member who passed due to illness. Together they have performed amazing healings for me, including eradicating migraine headaches, fixing torn ligaments and even completely healing a hernia in my abdomen - which allowed me to carry twins to full-term with no complications.

In addition to your spiritual team members who have never been part of your earthly family, your support system is likely also comprised of family members who have passed on. Anyone who has ever shown you love remains connected to you from the other side and can assist you with their particular special gifts. When a soul passes over, they often see things in a much different way than they did while on earth. Even if they were relatively unevolved here, all beings who die and make the *choice* to return to the Light, embrace the incredible power that is available there. They become one with the Creative Force of the Universe and embody the immense power of love that is a primary element of their new reality. In turn, they are happy to share it with you. These beings thrive on the opportunity to serve and are just a call away. Since they are no longer fettered by issues of form like time, space or matter, and since they oftentimes know us very well, they can have an incredibly profound effect on many of our mortal challenges.

Through continued communication and practice I have learned which of my team members excel in certain areas, and so can you. I can now sense who is available to bring the greatest energy needed in different circumstances. Some have exceptional skills in working with physical health issues, some in dealing with children's matters, others in marriage or relationship issues, still others in work related challenges or financial problems. When you start becoming aware of their presence, you begin to sense their particular areas of interest and how to call them forth. I know this is a difficult concept, but don't overthink it. It's more about being present in the moment with what they might be wanting to tell you. First and foremost, set an intention to maintain a relationship with them. Then, with practice, as you quiet your mind you can more easily learn how to communicate with them. They will always speak to you from the perspective of love, kindness, power, intelligence and oftentimes humor. Remain alert for signs and messages and they will come.

As you set your intention to hear them, they will help you do so. Asking questions is the best method to receive a response. Because they honor our free-will, they typically wait for an invitation and asking questions is an excellent way to get answers. Being specific with your question or request sends a strong energy beam, which is easy for them to pick up. Just like a radio signal, the stronger your signal, the better. Speaking your question or request out loud increases your energy signal and, although not required, I have found speaking to them out loud works exceptionally well in eliciting a clear and timely response.

A good method I use to open a channel for information is to think, "What are my team members wanting to say to me right now?" I then move my conscious mind out of the way by relaxing as I listen with all senses on "receive." When I was a child I had asthma. I used to have to get shots on a regular basis. It was during this time that I learned how to move my conscious mind "outside of myself" in order to ease my pain. I would close my eyes and focus more on my spiritual self than on my physical self. Similarly, in order to get clear messages from your team, you must focus more on them than on yourself. This places your consciousness in their arena. You will know a communication is from them, because it comes quickly and without effort. You can go about your normal day, but always work to keep part of your mind open to the fact that they are walking right beside you and messages and opportunities will be presented.

I once lost an earbud I loved. It was pink, one of my favorite colors, and connected via bluetooth to my cell phone. It was small and could easily disappear, which it had a couple times before. But each time I'd lost it, I'd been able to find it with very little effort. This time it had been lost for several days. I wanted it back and communicated this to my team. I opened my mind to listen and went about my day. Later, as I was walking into my bedroom closet, the phrase quickly and clearly came into my mind, "...between a rock and a hard place."

In that moment, my gaze shifted up to the left side of my closet where I had hung a wet green top to dry. This top has many different colored pebbles sewn around the collar. It was hanging in such a way as to face the opposite wall of the closet. In between the top and the opposite wall was a row of hanging clothes. I followed my line of vision (which your team will often direct when they know you are truly receptive) and saw a jacket I occasionally wore. I immediately realized I had to look in the pocket of that jacket. There, of course, it was. Safely tucked between a rock (the pebbles on the collar of my top) and a hard place (the wall) was my earbud. In that moment, I swore I could hear their soft chuckles.

Besides actual words, other ways your SST will communicate with you might include a song, picture, story or video that pops up in front of you. Or an idea that offers a solution to a dilemma. Or someone will cross your path to offer assistance or information that helps you with your challenge or need. Another way is a nagging thought. As I was writing this chapter I kept thinking about someone I know who is not genuine in her relationships. She tends to get close to people only who she feels can help her in some way. While I can have some compassion for this, it turns me off. I understand at a very fundamental level she is afraid of being alone, probably because she does not believe she has the strength to survive on her own. However, it is my responsibility not to allow myself to be used in such a manner. I kept wondering why I was even thinking about her. Then it hit me. My team was trying to get my attention to communicate this to you. They feel the very same way about us. It is imperative that our relationship with them be *genuine*. They want us to come together with them in order to experience a mutually enjoyable exchange, not because we need anything from them. Like the majority of us, they thrive in a satisfying give and take relationship. They'd also like you to know that you have much more strength and power than you realize. And, they enjoy watching you achieve connection with your own strength. This is, after all, one of the primary reasons you came forth. That said, your SST is available to assist you with your challenges and thrilled to offer you a creative flow of new ideas and solutions to problems. After all, we are *co-creators* with them in our life experience.

This flow of creativity can easily be achieved while performing any simple task that you enjoy. Doing so tends to move your critical, nay-saying, left brain out of the way. So while your rational left brain is busily distracted on a simple task, your team members can easily flow creative information to your right brain where it can be mulled over and expanded upon. Some people accomplish this while working on a hobby, cooking, jogging, or showering. Steve Jobs loved taking walks with friends while expressing his creative thoughts out loud. This was the way he connected with his team members for inspiration, whether or not he was aware of it.

Play around with what works best to encourage your SST to communicate ideas, solve problems or to just interact with you. Remember that they work best by invitation. Set a clear intention to receive information or a solution from them and it will come. When you have a problem that requires resolution, focus on receiving the solution, not on the problem itself. This is extremely important as it affects the energy you are sending out. And remember your team is either attracted, or not attracted, by your vibration. If you fixate on the problem, the stress you experience will block your ability to hear them. The angst you feel by focusing on the problem itself, rather than the solution, causes you to drape a sheath over yourself for protection. While this is natural, it works against your ability to receive your team's input. Work instead on calming yourself as much as possible and then set a strong intention for resolution.

My daughter had to wear retainers after having her braces removed. She has a tendency to leave them wrapped in bathroom tissue throughout the house. The retainers are clear and easy to lose, which she did this one night in particular. As we were searching for the third time, I spoke to my team members asking them to help. I told them I wanted her to see proof that they are real. Like most teens, she tends to not want to accept mom's beliefs about anything. As we were going through the large garbage can in our cold garage, I started to feel frustrated and get mad at her. Suddenly, I realized that was not the way I wanted to behave, so I decided to stop and instead began joking with her. As we both continued sorting through the wet mounds of garbage, I said, "Well, we do enjoy working on special projects together…" She laughed and so did I. Within about a minute, we found the plain white tissue they were wrapped in. This was even after she and her father had just meticulously combed through the same exact garbage can. I was happy to inform her that my spiritual team had played a role.

I realized that by releasing the stress and becoming playful, I had created the optimal environment for my team members to easily flow assistance into the situation. Like previously said, although they are with us in all situations, a focus on stress tends to make it more difficult for us to hear and receive their assistance. The fact remains that they are with us under all conditions and always work according to our overall set intention. However, it's easier for us to receive their assistance when we are in a more relaxed state.

As I said before, I do not worship them, but I have grown to love them. Our relationship is more of a brother and sister, peer to peer versus hierarchical type. I know this group is always with me and loves me unconditionally. It's a side benefit that our team members are able to deliver some incredibly powerful medicine. We share humor, ideas, and musings. They are with me in my joy, my frustration, my confusion, my wins and my losses. They help with many things, from letting me know when something is on sale in the grocery store to how to make a new dish for dinner to how to communicate more effectively with certain "challenging" individuals. They help me to be strong when I need to be. They assist me in understanding and forgiving people when necessary. They help me to realize when I need to walk away. They often bring me a friend to help with a particular problem when I need it. They provide exactly the right information that I need in certain situations. They help me remember things I need to know - like gentle nudges when I'm deep in conversation and not noticing that I need to pick up the kids from school. They have awakened me in the middle of the night when I needed to be aware of danger. They have a wonderful sense of humor and are never judgmental of me. While they will not interfere with our predestined challenges - as those are opportunities for our personal growth - our team members can help us in many ways. As you will find, the more you practice engaging them, even under stress, the more miracles will demonstrate themselves to you.

I once had a throat infection when my regular doctor was out of town. So, I had to be seen by a different overworked, grouchy physician who clearly wanted to be doing anything else than attending to another doctor's patients. He quickly checked me out and hastily wrote me a prescription for a name brand name antibiotic which was new on the market and had no generic equivalent. When I went to the pharmacy, I was told the drug would not be covered by my insurance plan and my co-pay would be over $150. I was unwilling to pay that for a few pills, so I returned to the doctor's office. I explained to the receptionist that I would like the doctor to write me a prescription for a generic antibiotic, which I had used in the past instead. I was left waiting for about half an hour before I decided to approach the receptionist again. I asked her if she would please check on the doctor's progress in writing me the new prescription. While she was gone, I whispered to my team, telling them I needed their intervention and that it was my intention to receive help in this situation. Within a few minutes the nurse appeared with a bag for me containing all the medication I needed...free of charge...with an apology. Not by the harried doctor, but by another physician who had intervened, obviously directed by "other-worldly forces" to resolve my problem.

Even though stressful situations used to cause me to put up an emotional wall for protection, I've now learned to try to relax and to immediately call in my SST instead of just working to protect myself. I have seen amazing things happen by doing this and I have no doubt you will, too. The key is to concentrate on the result you wish to obtain, over and above the stress you're feeling in the moment. Call them in, thank them for their presence and tell them what you want to see happen. I have seen this process work miracles. Conversely, I've also experienced disastrous results when I've forgotten to employ it.

Although we will not always get what we want in every situation, as challenges are a part of life, there is *always* a gift in what we do get. The trick is to find it. The other day I slipped and fell down several steps in my house. My entire body was scraped from one end to the other and I was sore for several days. I decided that every time I thought about how painful my fall had been, I would immediately follow-up by feeling grateful it had not been worse. It is my plan to continue this practice through to the day I die. I have studied a multitude of accounts of people who have passed over and told their stories about life on the other side. I know there is something incredible and awesomely beautiful which awaits us there. So, even though there will be painful situations on this side of the veil of life, I know it is possible to find the gift of opportunity in everything. The Source of Life has given us this short time on earth to experience all good and bad as a wonderful opportunity to see ourselves as the strong and courageous souls we truly are. And, that is a huge gift.

In her description of her Spiritual Support Team, Natalie Sudman said, *The only limitation that I perceive in regards to the actions of these personalities, and the limitation is voluntary, is that they always act in support of the intentions of the individual that they are assisting.*

Holding our intention for triumph strongly in the midst of a stressful situation is nothing short of an incredibly awesome skill. But that is one of the things we came forth to practice. In observing those who routinely demonstrate a strong intention for success, I've noticed that a bit of attitude seems to go a long way. I'm obviously not talking about a negative attitude. But, rather a strong and powerful resolve that says, "This is how I'm expecting this situation to work out. I know I am incredibly valuable and I know the energies surrounding me are supportive of me. This truth is what I am standing in and nothing else." This attitude sits on the edge of entitlement, but does not utilize force, which would cause stress and drive away the positive energies you are trying to attract. It is a type of powerful, positive self-love. I suggest we learn to hold that type of firm belief of our deservedness as we go throughout our day, especially when we are faced with challenges. Communicate powerfully, with all the faith filled energy you have that you know your team members have

52

your back and you trust they are going to show up for you in the best way possible.

Just as Natalie Sudman's own spiritual team members promised her they would always remain with her and would be continuously accessible, our own team has made the same commitment to us. In order to receive support from them, we *must ask* - preferably out loud - *knowing* that we deserve, while *believing* they are here for us, that they have our backs and will support us through whatever we are going through. We do well never to lose sight of the fact that we are spiritual warriors armed with the knowledge that a mighty God serves us and that together we came forth to win!

Chapter 5
The Tape

Like a lot of people, there were times in my past when I used to pray only when I needed something or when things were falling apart in my life. When things were going well, making an effort and finding time for connecting with God was not the highest priority on my list, to say the least. In my twenties and even into my mid-thirties, although I knew about my spirituality from my past experiences, I didn't consciously work on maintaining a daily connection like I do now. Needless to say, those years of my life carried a lot of emptiness and even a constant ache, somewhat akin to a feeling of abandonment. In reality, it was me who had abandoned the very essence of my own life force. At a very deep level, I had abandoned myself. I had put my soul in the care of other people and the world around me, which is a very dangerous thing to do.

It was during one of these empty periods in my life, when I was especially low, that the divine beings who surround us performed a remarkably awesome feat of love and support. Nothing was necessarily wrong, but nothing was right either. My dad had died a few years earlier, I have no siblings and my mother and I had never had a close relationship, so I couldn't count on her for anything, except ridicule. I had just broken up with a man I'd been dating for a long time and I didn't have much of a social life. Work was okay, but it didn't provide the emotional fulfillment or support I needed. I was depressed and felt alone.

I remember driving home from work to my empty apartment with an especially heavy heart, week after week...especially on Fridays when I knew I'd be facing another solitary weekend. There was one thing I never gave up on, however, and that was my pursuit of my connection with God the Divine, albeit only on Sundays only. I continued attending church, at that time the Palo Alto Unity Church, and half-heartedly explored different ways to grow spiritually.

On this evening, like most others, I prepared my dinner and took it into the living room to eat on the coffee table in front of the television set, which was my routine. As soon as I sat down on the floor, I realized I hadn't poured my nightly glass of wine (which itself was probably not the best ritual). Anyway, I got up and walked back into the kitchen.

I had not been gone from the kitchen for more than a minute or two. There, sitting squarely on the dishrag I had just been using, right next to the refrigerator was a cassette tape (cassette because this was 1991). I had not seen this particular tape since probably 1984, when I had purchased it following a spiritual lecture I'd attended. The tape was turned to side B and positioned in such a manner on the dishrag as to make it clear it had been purposely placed that way, specifically for me to see. Side B was the 7 Terrace Meditation by Paul Solomon.

I immediately became frightened and began calling everyone I could think of who might help me figure out how that tape, which I hadn't seen for years, came to appear in my kitchen. I knew something or someone was in that kitchen with me. I was an occasional smoker at the time and remember fervently chain smoking cigarettes during my phone calls in an effort to "drive it away." I must have ridiculously figured whoever it was in spirit that was visiting me would be offended by the smell of cigarette smoke and go away. Thinking back on the beings that had gathered and were standing around me at that moment, they must have surely been laughing hysterically through the clouds of smoke.

Interestingly, I was able to get ahold of everyone I called, including the psychic who had originally sold me the tape in the first place. As I recounted the story of what had just happened in my kitchen, he was not shocked, nor did he sound doubtful about what I was telling him.

I remember asking him who he thought might have put the tape there and he said, matter-of-factly, "Well, it was your Guidance." I wasn't quite sure what that meant, but assumed it was a divine being and was satisfied with that answer. He was a very gifted psychic who had previously told me many things about my past, which only I would have known. Looking back, I wish he had elaborated in that moment and instead of using the words "your guidance," said something like, "Well Adriana, it was your Guidance Team, a group of spiritual beings who is always with you and who will do anything they can to support you. Now you see that they are very real and powerful and incredibly anxious to help you. So engage them, talk with them, ask them for whatever you need and, as you believe, you will receive."

A clear explanation like that would have saved me years of wandering around the desert lost, having to take the long road into my final realization that we are always surrounded by such powerful entities. Nonetheless, the entire episode left me exhilarated, albeit shaken. When I finally calmed down, I realized whoever or whatever it was had been trying to tell me something...indeed It seemed to be trying to help me. To work to demonstrate such power as to go through walls in order to leave me a mediation tape was not just astounding, but incredibly sweet and caring! I wondered if they had to obtain special permission to perform such a miracle.

The tape, by the way, had been stored for years inside a shoebox on the highest shelf of the cupboard located above my refrigerator. This cupboard was always kept closed and was unreachable without a stool. When I looked around, I noticed nothing had been left open or disturbed. That is, except for the cassette tape which was now lying, B side up, on top of the dishrag on the counter. The cupboard door was still completely closed and looked as if it had never been opened. Something very powerful was indeed trying to tell me something.

So, I began to listen to the tape. It was a guided meditation, which leads you to tranquil surroundings. It then leads you to a room where you can talk to whomever in spirit you wish. Or you can choose to go to another room where you can access the Akashic records. These are the recordings of everything that ever was or will ever be. These are the records that truly gifted psychics are able to access when performing readings.

In the weeks that followed, I sat and went through the meditation probably a total of five times. But, since I've never been a big meditator (especially back then) or a very patient person, I soon tired of it and quit. I decided whoever my visitor was that evening they must be trying to tell me I should again focus on developing my psychic skills. I started doing readings for people in my spare time and soon realized that my new hobby was making me happy which, no doubt, was the intention of the entire episode. Since then I've realized they were also seeking a greater connection with me. Part of the purpose of a guided meditation, which relaxes your mind and opens your heart, is to make yourself more inviting and someone who is easier to communicate with.

To this day, I am not sure if my visitor that evening was a team member, a larger group of beings or if it was my father who had passed on a couple years earlier. My dad and I had an especially close relationship and I knew he loved me very much. Perhaps my dad is one of my team members. It doesn't matter. I knew then, as I know now, that I was extremely blessed to have had such an awesome experience. This should demonstrate to anyone reading this, whether or not you've had such an obvious show of support from your own SST, that we are *all* loved by other-worldly beings who will do whatever they can to assist us in finding peace and joy.

Chapter 6
Imperfectly Perfect

I had just moved to a new town and met a group of women. We decided to meet regularly to go for walks on a local hiking trail. After a few months, a couple of the girls invited in two new ladies. One woman only joined our get-togethers once. She told me she had encountered issues with her friend Gloria (the other newcomer) flirting with her husband. I didn't pay much attention to this, as everyone has their own experiences with people. However, one day soon after she'd joined our group, Gloria followed me to my car following a group luncheon.

There she began to tell me about an affair she was having with a married man. I'm not sure why she was telling me all this and I certainly wasn't enjoying listening to it. I left as soon as I could manage an excuse to exit. But after this incident she would periodically try to regale me with stories of the doctor she was seeing behind her husband's back whenever she could corner me. Interestingly, she would never mention her affair when the other women were around. I had met her husband and he seemed to be a very nice person, as were her two young daughters. Needless to say, her persistent story-telling of her sexual encounters left me nauseous. Each time she cornered me, I couldn't wait to escape. I told her she was risking losing her family if her husband ever discovered her indiscretions and that, since no man is perfect, she should be happy with what she had. This advice fell on deaf ears, as evidenced by her subsequent eye rolling.

I love the joy of Halloween and especially seeing my children having fun. On one of our walks, I mentioned to my friends wanting to give my daughter a Halloween party, but wasn't sure if I actually would since she was now getting older. Flirty Gloria immediately piped up and said her daughters would love a party and that we could have it at her house. I hesitantly agreed.

I should have paid attention to that intuitive feeling I had which said, "What are you doing?!" because that party ended up being a disaster. Gloria had told me her husband would be there, so I invited mine. She greeted us at the door wearing a short lace nightie with matching pom pom high heeled slippers. I later discovered that she and her husband had been arguing and he had stormed out before we arrived. With no other male in attendance, my husband looked especially uncomfortable sitting there wearing the clown outfit I'd suggested would be fun.

As the children started to arrive, I asked Gloria when she planned to change into her costume. She proudly announced that she was already wearing it! I rarely say things I regret, but I'm thinking perhaps because Mercury was in Retrograde, I then made an unfortunate comment about her looking like a slut - which I would later come to regret. To make a long story short I used a word which, however aptly described her appearance, was not the nicest thing I could have said. I spent the rest of the evening focusing on the children, as I usually do at Halloween parties. I noticed each time my husband would go to the restroom he'd return wearing less of the clown outfit until he was back in street clothes. Gloria and a couple of friends who had arrived after my slut comment, spent the remainder of the evening drinking in another room, which was fine with me.

Following that party, I wisely decided it would not be in my best interest to spend any more time around Gloria. Our friends, none of whom were in attendance at the party that evening, did not agree with my decision, insinuating I was being too judgmental. So, I again ignored my inner voice and went to a subsequent group get-together where she was in attendance. Almost immediately, Gloria brought up the Halloween party incident while the entire group was seated around the table. She employed impressive dramatics, clutching her heart while describing me as being rude and insensitive. In horror, I sat staring at her like a deer caught in headlights, not quite knowing what to say, except that I realized I never wanted to be around her again.

Incredibly, my friends continued inviting both Gloria and myself to gatherings together. With some sadness, but extreme clarity regarding my need for peace, I made the decision that I would rather be true to my own intentions than part of a group. Therefore, I decided I would need to gracefully distance myself from them if I was going to have the peace of mind I deserved.

The entire thing was unfortunate and I was not pleased with the turn of events, but I also did not harbor any anger towards anyone. I was mainly disappointed in the situation itself and its outcome. But, I was strong and clear in my intention that I deserve positive and mutually supportive relationships in my life and that is where I'm going to place my energy. So I went on with my life, although I dreaded the possibility of running into Gloria again.

Looking back, I realize the group had been taking a lot of my time. We would typically walk for 3 miles 5 days per week, leaving little time for anything else. I actually prefer to run every other day, but had forsaken that practice in deference to camaraderie. Also, the members did not share my spiritual understandings, so I didn't feel comfortable discussing them. Leaving the group allowed me to have enough time to start writing this book and to be more truly who I really am...which was likely my soul's larger intention.

A few weeks after making the decision to move on, I was in the Target store near my home with my daughter. It is a rather large store and I was in an aisleway near housewares. Some distance away, about 80 feet, but still in my view, was the front door.

Suddenly, I felt "something" distinctly shift my attention in that direction. I quickly looked over and saw two people sitting on a bench by the main entrance. I didn't think anything of it and started to shift my attention away. But, whoever or whatever it was that I felt standing next to me, urged me look back. It felt like a soft, yet unmistakable tap on my shoulder. This time, when I looked in that direction again, my gaze landed on two figures seated on the bench. Looking closer, I realized it was Gloria and her husband.

If I had gone out that door, the way I was planning to, a very uncomfortable situation would have certainly occurred. At that moment, I KNEW beyond a shadow of a doubt, that there is something very real, who looks out for us. And, in a very non-judgmental, supportive and loving way, this something has our backs. All we need to do is pay attention. And pay *a lot* of attention.

It's interesting to note that several months prior to this incident I had, in earnest, started studying about Angels with Doreen Virtue. The "tap" on my shoulder to get me to look in the direction of the front door was very subtle...almost like the touch of a feather. However, the presence next to me was undeniable. It was strong and it was obviously looking out for me. Like many I've been blessed with, I will never forget that incredible day.

Establishing this connection does not insure our lives will be free from pain or discomfort or that we will get everything we want. This is, after all, planet earth. We came forth to experience a multitude of situations. We volunteered and agreed (although it may not feel like it at times) to participate in certain challenges before we incarnated here.

As previously stated, the challenges we encounter on earth provide excellent learning opportunities for the growth of our own soul. Which, in turn, promote the growth of Universal Intelligence as a whole. That said, maintaining a relationship with our SST through it all definitely makes our life a lot sweeter and oftentimes less arduous.

In the end, I decided to send a note to Gloria asking for her forgiveness. I realized I had a lot of better things to do with my energy than waste it worrying about running into her and I'm sure my team members did as well. Plus, I've always enjoyed participating in the extreme spiritual sport of forgiveness. I call it that, because not many people practice it and fewer still do it well. I'm in the constant state of learning how to perfect it myself, for to do so carries it's own rewards. I feel expressing compassion and understanding is important and I was given that opportunity - towards both Gloria and myself. Because, obviously, I wasn't completely innocent in the turn of events. In any case, since peace and contentment remains my strong intention for my life, I felt that asking for her forgiveness would free up my energy and bring me the peace I deserved as I move around our small town. Letting go of that situation lifted a weight off me which was unhealthy to be carrying around and the entire incident provided me with an incredibly valuable experience.

Even though I had not behaved perfectly in this situation, it was revealed beyond a shadow of a doubt that my team still had my back. Proof that our SST members are non-judgmental and don't dole out favors only to those who achieve perfection. Again - we don't have to be perfect, just perfectly available. Available to the awareness that we are not alone. None of us is. We are all surrounded by a special group of spiritual beings who adore us and who will do whatever they can, given our level of awareness, to improve our life on earth.

I don't care if you are a sweet monk in a temple or a hardened criminal behind bars, you have a powerful team of spiritual beings who are constantly on your side. Practice engaging them, interact with them, talk to them, ask them questions, listen to their whispered guidance and look for signs. You must listen not just with your mind, but with your heart, while keeping your eyes open for signs of their presence. And, most importantly, you must ask...always ask for guidance and input.

The fact is, we are *all* unconditionally loved, no matter what, and my experience in Target that day proves it.

Chapter 7
Greatest Love

I used to love going to a fruit stand near the beach when I lived in Santa Cruz. I was attending a Spiritual Practitioner course at the time and my newfound awareness of God in our daily lives was blossoming. They played beautiful love songs over the sound-system at this fruit stand. There in the middle of mountains of fresh fruit and vegetables with sea-breezes softly caressing my face, I felt a magnificent sense of oneness with everything around me. Among the sweet scent of apples and peaches, I fell in love with the moment. I suddenly realized I was an integral part of this awesome creation called life. Even though I didn't realize it then, this "being-in-oneness-with-the-moment" creates the perfect environment for our team to send us strong communications. The heightened awareness alone is a message from them saying, "Isn't it all so beautiful? And we're right here to share it with you." One day as a love song came on the speakers and melded sweetly into my already overflowing sense of awe, I suddenly realized the love songs were being sung to me!

In that moment, I came to the realization that these songs of love were being offered to me from my own awesome soul! Our soul is the heart of our expanded self, which resides primarily in the non-physical. Our soul is an integral part of our SST, providing leadership by maintaining a strong presence in both the physical and non-physical realms. From then on, every time I would enter that fruit stand and hear those beautiful love songs, I knew they were being sung especially to me from the heart of my own sacred self.

Those sweet experiences were the start of something huge. I learned then that the greatest lesson we can ever learn is the magnitude of power that is contained in the practice of self love. You can't really move on to anything else until you've mastered this basic first step.

I'm not talking about short-sighted selfishness here. In contrast to selfishness, self love seeks to flow love through the self and out toward others and the world around us. In that way, self love is cleansing and energizing. And flowing love is what we came forth to do. So while selfishness cuts off the life force, choking it in an attempt to hoard it, self love enables the life force, pulling forth more energy as it flows outward. People who don't understand this are walking around everyday thinking they are practicing self love, when indeed it is selfishness they exhibit and they remain confused as to why they still feel a deep emptiness.

The flow of the life force must be allowed to spring forth from within you or its massive energy will choke your very spirit. Love cannot be hoarded, it was made to be shared with others and the world around you. Flowing love towards others and into the world is like a river. The stronger the river flows, the more it pulls from its source. This Source of Life is inexhaustible and It loves to be summoned.

When you practice true self love, you aren't as prone to engaging in certain self-defeating behaviors. When you truly love and respect yourself, you realize that responding to someone else with anger, cruelty or hatred only makes you, yourself, feel bad. No matter how inappropriate their behavior, you begin to look inside yourself for understanding. You realize that understanding a situation leads to compassion. You seek to practice compassion, because that is what allows the awesome experience of love to flow through you without hindrance. And you come to realize there is nothing more important.

You understand that to love feels much better than to express anger or hate. You realize that you don't want to be the one responsible for making yourself feel bad. You become more aware of how you feel and how to want to feel. You begin to choose your own thoughts, and the things you give your attention to, more wisely. You make a choice that you are going to work to feel as good as possible in whatever situation or under whatever circumstances you happen to be in.

Along with anger and hatred, resentment is another self-defeating emotional practice. Although your hurt may indeed be justified, holding on to and letting it fester beyond a healthy moment of self-expression, does not feel good. It eats away at your sense of peace, your well-being and ultimately,

71

your self-worth. Resentment attacks your self-worth, because you are more focused your anger with the other person or situation than you are on your own happiness. You are giving away your power to them and, in turn, not honoring or valuing yourself above all else... and that feels bad.

Harboring resentment, anger or hatred gets in the way of our connection with ourselves and our spiritual team members. It creates a type of isolation and static, so that our connection with our team is weakened. It then becomes harder for them to hear what we're saying we really want. Are we saying we're resigned to living in hatred, anger and pain? Are we saying we are powerless in the situation? If so, that will be honored. Or are we saying we're strong and ready to move on towards a more positive experience? They will honor our intention, no matter what we are putting forth. That is the power of our focus and it is why clearing resentment from our hearts is so important. It creates a clear connection between you and your team that says, "My intention is to have an awesome life experience, no matter what."

Practicing self love also frees you from carrying negative vibrations. Negative vibrations attract negative energy. Of course, it is unreasonable to expect that you will be positive all the time, neither is it healthy, as we must be true to our feelings. However, a chronic lack of self love attracts unevolved, lower "earthbound energies" that will actually fuel those negative emotions. If you carry resentment, for example, you will actually attract unevolved spirits who also harbor resentment. This is extremely dangerous. You see it all the time. People who go around chronically angry require little to get angrier still. That is because they are being fueled from those unevolved spirits who have rejected the Light of God and who themselves harbor unresolved anger and resentment.

Earthbound spirits are people who have passed on, but refuse to leave this earthly realm. They are stuck in-between worlds. They still carry hate, unresolved anger and/or unforgiveness. They have refused to go toward the Light and the Light, in It's incredible wisdom and benevolence, always honors free will. The Light, although much more powerful than any negative energies, will never force anyone to come to It. Those spirits will not move on until they choose to forgive and embrace their own sense of self love. The concept of self love and forgiveness is foreign to them, because they didn't practice it when they were alive. Therefore, heaven would - for them - be hell.

This is why it is imperative that you never buy into the untruth that you are anything less than a sacred being, incredibly worthy of the grandest love and support from you yourself, as well as from the Beings of Light who surround you. You must become like a spiritual warrior and always work to stave off any erroneous feelings of unworthiness. To give into a feeling of unworthiness is to abandon yourself. When you abandon yourself to negative energies, you become attractive to earthbound spirits and they will swoop in to fuel your sense of worthlessness as they feed off of this energy. This phenomenon is similar to the way humans are attracted to one another. Complainers can often be found hanging in groups of other complainers. Angry people love to hang out with other angry people, because doing so fuels their unevolved energy.

If you make a habit of living in the lower vibrations of anger, resentment or hopelessness you will provide fuel to these energies and they will move in closer, becoming louder and edging out the Light Beings who want to help you. This is why you must remain vigilant and spiritually strong. Allowing self love to be your shield, focus on the wonderful beings of the Light of God who surround you. Doing so calls them forth and they are much stronger than any dark energies. Dark energies cannot stand the brightness of your heavenly support team. Their powerful light automatically repels them. However, the Light will always honor your free will. You must demonstrate your desire to live in the light of love and compassion, which is where they reside. The Light is always stronger than the dark, but it must be beckoned by your positive and decisive vibration. Self love is such a vibration and it is key to your being a walking/breathing child of the Light. Self love and its brother, self-forgiveness, are basic requirements for living in the Light. They empower you on every level.

An important aspect of self love is embracing your personal power, especially in relationships. This does not mean lording it over the other person, but rather to be in balance with them. Many years ago I read a line in Neale Donald Walsch's book, "Conversations with God," that has stayed with me. God, through Neale, said, "I do not demonstrate my love for you by not allowing you to demonstrate your love for me." That simple, yet incredibly profound statement has helped me to understand that I must also give others the opportunity to demonstrate love and compassion back to me. That is really loving them. To "do it all" in relationship with another person does not demonstrate my love for them, as I am not letting them have the chance to generate love within themselves. I am, in effect, robbing them of the opportunity to be who they are, a child of God who was meant to be a blessing to themselves and to others. We came to earth to experience ourselves as people who have the power to generate love. Stealing that opportunity from someone is actually an unkind thing to do. Coming to the realization that to love "in balance" is the true definition of the word. It is one of the most liberating understandings you can ever hope to achieve.

Real self love is the true honoring of the sacred Divinity of Life that we are each a part of. That Divinity flows through us, to the degree of our invitation, delivering awesome power into our lives. Once you attain self love, you will never lose it. Even if you lose sight of it for a moment, like a sweet memory, it will always find its way back home to your heart. It can only grow deeper. It opens the door to the part of your heart which believes in magic and invites miracles.

Chapter 8
The Gift

Pam Grout has written several books on attracting incredible adventures and manifestations into our lives. It was the fall of 2013 when I read her first book, E-Squared. In it, she outlines several experimentations which can be done to summon what she calls the Field of Possibility (or FP for short). As I interpret it, the term FP describes what quantum physicists now understand to be the existence of a field, or quantum web, which connects everything. Within this field lies infinite possibilities.

When I read E-Squared, I was not yet aware of my spiritual team to the degree that I am now. However, I was strongly aware that there was some sort of powerful something at work in my life and I was anxious to learn how to interact with it.

Pam's bold experiments, intended to call forth the power within the infinite field, fascinated me. I couldn't wait to get started. So, on the evening of September 19, 2013 at 10:50 p.m. I eagerly began Experiment #1, called the Dude Abides Principle. We were directed to conduct the experiment over a 72 hour period in a scientific manner utilizing an official looking Lab Report Sheet. This Lab Report outlines the Theory, Hypothesis, Research Notes and Results of our experiment. I was ready, anxious and very excited. I made the decision that if the experiment bore no fruit within 72 hours, it was just a timing issue and that I'd repeat my experiment until it was successful. I just knew it would eventually work. But, I didn't want to put any undue stress on myself nor "the field". I felt I was being pretty bold, but I was ready.

In order to get the full effect of what happened in this experiment, a little background on me is helpful. I am an only child and was abandoned when I was 12 years old. My mother left me with some strangers when my dad was on yet another of his mysteriously long vacations by himself. Bless her heart, my mother was never cut out to be a parent. She was always very uncomfortable in the role of mother. Coupled with my father often taking month long vacations to Mexico without her during the school year when she'd be forced to stay at home with me, a lot was stacked against my being able to have a normal childhood. I have done a lot of forgiveness work around this and can now see my mom with great compassion and understanding. This explanation is for the purposes of your getting a clear picture of the magnitude of what I'm about to tell you. I was born to my parents late in life, my mom was 41 and my father was 50. This, coupled with fact that I had no siblings, meant I had no close family members after my dad died in 1989.

Even though I now have children of my own, I always longed to have other adult family members. I did have two cousins, but we weren't close since they moved to the other end of California when I was about 8 years old. Although we exchanged Christmas cards, we'd fallen out of touch over the years, as people who haven't seen each other since childhood often do. Prior to this experiment, I had recently heard from one of them who said she'd been researching our family tree following the death of her mother. She said she had uncovered some interesting information about our Native-American roots, but that was about all she had discovered.

My experiment began on September 19, 2013 at 10:50 p.m., which was a Thursday. That meant the FP only had until Saturday evening to deliver. Earlier that day I had received a voice message from my cousin in Southern California, but had gotten busy and didn't get the chance to return the call right away.

Saturday evening came and went with no miracle. Instead of being disappointed, I clearly remember my decision to give it another try and decided to continue waiting. Early Monday morning I realized I still hadn't returned the call to my cousin. So, out on the trail during my morning walk, I called her on my cell phone. I had a Facebook page, but my cousin did not. So she directed me to search for a name she had uncovered during her research of someone she believed was in our family who lives in Bakersfield. I did so while I had her on the line. When the person's profile popped up on my screen, a blast of adrenaline shot right through me.

"Oh my God! It's your dad!" I cried in shock. Before me was a picture taken in the 1940s of her now deceased father, my uncle Paul, standing with my aunt Esther who I'd both been close to. They were with another man (whom I'd later learn was my uncle Mike, who I'd never met) and some children. The person who had posted the picture was our cousin Ernest, who neither she nor I had ever met. Her family tree digging had led her to him and one other family member. I immediately "friended" my newly found cousin Ernest and the other Dominguez family member from Santa Barbara. I sent them a note explaining who I was and how I had located them.

Within half an hour they had not just friended me back, but "suggested" a list of about 40 other Dominguez cousins and second cousins of mine. These are people I didn't even know existed prior to embarking on this experiment. For the previous 10 years, since my aunt Mary passed on, I had thought I had no other living adult relatives. Within another few minutes, I had connected with most of them. The emotion reliving this story as I'm writing it now, is still overwhelming. This was definitely an incredible and undeniable miracle for me. True proof of the existence of what I have now come to know as a group of extremely powerful beings who surround us constantly, love us immensely and work according to our focused intention.

Had I returned my cousin's phone call earlier, the experiment would have ended well within the allotted time-frame of 72 hours. Following are my notes from it:

Absolutely Amazing! At first I thought FP hadn't delivered, but it was me who hadn't followed up on a lead that I had been presented with. In the end I was given over 40 family members I didn't know I had!

Over the past few years I have enjoyed wonderful family get-togethers, camping trips and awesome parties with my newly discovered cousins. For me, this was a miracle of epic proportions, one for which I will forever be grateful and in awe. I mean, seriously, a family where before there had been none? That is nothing short of miraculous!

Did everyone who performed this experiment have similar results? No. But, many did. You can find details of my own experience briefly summarized at the bottom of page 60 in Pam Grout's subsequent book, E-Cubed. I was so happy and excited about it, I think I told everyone I knew, including Pam. She was kind enough to include it in the list of incredible results several of her other readers had also achieved.

I believe everyone can experience results when there is something you have been longing for with significant focused intention aimed towards it. Especially, if you simultaneously hold appreciation toward yourself and your SST. Initially, the intention to receive the gift sends the request. Subsequently, the amount of focus expended towards the anticipation of the result itself, rather than on how it feels not to have it, generates the trust necessary for our team to take creative action. Focusing on results (i.e. having faith) creates clarity. And finally, as Pam put it, the level of *consciousness* you possess is the final determining factor in the success of any summoning exercise. Being conscious of our Spiritual Support Team and of our own divine nature opens up a channel for the incredible exchange of energies between worlds.

As I sat around the hotel pool with my newfound family members, a few weeks later, two of my cousins began discussing their experiences living overseas while in the service. Seems they had both done a tour in Germany and had picked up a bit of the language. Suddenly my cousin Gary said to my cousin Leonard, "Yeah, remember "Was ist los?" I was shocked to hear him say those words! Leonard responded, "Right, that means what's happening. Was ist los!" The two of them chuckled, while I sat dumbfounded. For years I had been researching that phrase, but I didn't have the correct spelling.

In quiet moments, I sometimes hear a soft spoken phrase pass through my mind. More often than not, it comes as a string of words sounding much like my own thoughts. But since I don't consciously think of the words myself, I've come to know it is my team speaking to me. For several years, I would periodically hear a phrase that sounded like "Vas es las?" in my mind. I began typing it into the internet to try and decipher what it meant, but could never find the translation, so I gave up. However, on this day sitting around the pool, I realized I was spelling the phrase incorrectly. You see, I had been typing the words phonetically. More importantly, my cousins knew what the phrase meant! Amazingly, it was a phrase that had been uttered to me by my SST for years. They had periodically been asking me "What's happening? What's going on with you?" In that moment I knew they had also been setting up this awesome moment for incredible confirmation, when my own cousins would repeat a phrase that only I could have known the significance of. A loving inquiry which had been uttered by my SST, into my ear so many times before.

Are they real? You betcha! Are they awesome! I have absolutely no doubt. Do they care about you? More than you could ever know. Are they available to you? Yes, especially if you are available to them. Remember, love in balance. Are they listening to you? The answer is a question, "Are you listening to them?"

Chapter 9
Graduation Day

In the spring of 2006, I was chosen to speak at the Commencement Exercises for my graduating class of Spiritual Practitioners. My presentation board consisted of a drawing, which outlined the various steps we'd all gone through on our path to spiritual growth. I noted that in the beginning my fellow classmates and I were all a bit indifferent to embarking on the job of spiritual enlightenment. For the most part we preferred to think the principles of spirituality such as kindness, compassion, and forgiveness were meant for people around us who needed to change - not us. Then slowly we all started to listen until we began to realize we each had a trunkload of unhealed issues in our own hearts. We did the work, which at times was tough, but it eventually allowed us to embrace our divine essence.

At the end of my presentation, I closed by saying that the work of clearing the storage bins of past issues in our hearts never stops, but remains an ongoing process. This is because the storage bin in our hearts was never meant to be a storage bin, but rather a beautiful fountain which was meant to be kept clean. I've since lost the lovely sparkly fountain my daughter helped me create using glitter and paste, which I used to cover the nasty looking storage bin on the center of that board at the end of my speech. But I will always remember the standing ovation my classmates and the audience gave me and my simple visual.

Back in my seat following a few more words of wisdom from our minister, all graduating class members were asked to stand in the pews and slowly come forward. One by one we were each called up to the altar to receive our diplomas. As the crowd began to applaud for each of my classmates and it came close to my own moment to walk up to the stage for my diploma, I started hearing several voices near me praying the Unity Prayer for Protection. It is a beautiful blessing. We weren't in a Unity Church at the time, but apparently that didn't matter. As the first couple of voices started to pray, I assumed some audience members from above me in the balcony must be praying out loud. But when I looked up, there was no one sitting in the balcony. However, the number and sound of the voices continued to grow in intensity. From above my head I could plainly hear each voice reciting the prayer, as their loudness and number of voices continued to grow, I could distinctly make out both male and female voices. Their words were clearly audible and nearly drowned out the din of the applause in the room. They weren't perfectly in unison, but they were easy to understand. It was the most beautiful sound I had ever heard. They loudly and clearly were speaking the blessing over me! "May the Light of God surround you, the Love of God enfold you, the Power of God protect you, the Presence of God watch over you. Wherever you are, God is." Over and over the voices prayed. They prayed that sweet prayer in it's entirety, probably a total of about five or six times.

Then my name was called. The group of voices began to grow quieter and by the time I reached the stage, they had stopped altogether. As I approached her, the minister handed me my diploma, smiled and greeted me by saying, "Reverend Adriana." At that time "Reverend" was not my official title. However, I took it as something she felt moved to say in the moment. Her blessing, along with what I had just heard from my glorious SST, served as impetus for me to continue my spiritual path.

Even though I never shared what happened that day with anyone except my husband, until now, that event marked an historic day for me. It was the only time that I have so loudly and clearly heard my team members voices. Even though I have hoped that they would again speak to me with such audible clarity, it has never happened exactly the way it did that day. However, they do communicate with me in much more subtle ways all the time. I feel incredibly blessed to have had that experience and will cherish it in my heart forever.

A couple years ago when I was researching the origins of that Prayer for Protection, I ran across the following story on the main Unity website. It seems James Dillet Freeman; poet, scholar and elder of the Unity movement had an experience almost identical to mine when the words to the prayer came to him. His detailed story was recently deleted from the Unity website and what remains is what, I suspect, is a more simplified explanation of how the prayer came to be. But I was able to locate some of the words I first read recently on a Facebook page developed by Silent Unity, the Unity Church's prayer arm. The posting dated June 11, 2014 is as follows:

"I had gone to pray for Katherine in the Silent Unity prayer room at 917 Tracy in Kansas City. As I sat there in agony, unable to bring my mind into enough order to speak words of prayer, suddenly I heard a voice. The voice was so real, so audible that I looked around to see who was there. The voice

said, "Do you need Me? I am there." As I sat there, the voice
continued... " - James Dillet Freeman.

In the complete version I'd originally read, he went on to say he always wished he could once again hear the voice, loud and audible as he had on that day. However, like me, he never did. He first wrote the prayer, I Am There, which came as a result of the words his Spiritual Team spoke aloud to him that day. Out of that, came the Prayer for Protection, which my own Spiritual Team spoke over me during my graduation ceremony. This Prayer for Protection was written by him in 1947 as the result of a request made for soldiers heading off to war. It is an extremely powerful prayer and is still prayed at the closing of most Unity Church services today.

I believe the reason I was able to hear my team members so loud and clear that day was because I'd gotten their attention by making a significant effort towards my spiritual growth. I'd made a commitment to follow through with doing the work of uncovering God's presence in my life and hadn't given up. I'd made a commitment to removing any blockages that were hindering my connection to my own beautiful soul and I'd stuck with it. That is a commitment I continue to make each and every day...and I will never give up. They were obviously pleased and offered me that blessing as a gift, a "thank you for your work."

Whether or not you ever actually hear your Spiritual Team members voices, be aware that they are extremely real and are constantly communicating with you. Make a concerted effort to hear them and you will, even if it is just a whisper into your mind. Make an effort to notice the blessings they constantly send and you will begin to see them in abundance, no matter what circumstances you find yourself in. If they are trying or difficult circumstances, work to view that as an opportunity, not a punishment. As you begin your search in earnest, make it a daily habit to offer appreciation for each of the small miracles you do experience each day. The more you rise to the challenge of keeping your attention on the connection between yourself and your team, the more you will experience blessings that present themselves in a variety of forms.

Chapter 10
The Fruits

In Spiritual Practitioner Class we were being taught that "the fruits are the result of the work." As I was standing in the restroom alone before class one morning at Zelda's Restaurant in Capitola thinking of all the "work" I had been doing, I said to God, "If you're all that and a bag of chips, show me a sign." Shortly afterwards, I'd all but forgotten my dare, as I walked out of the restroom to the cup of hot coffee that was waiting for me at the Barista's counter. I handed the girl my stamp card (10th cup free) with my money, as was my routine. She put the money in the register then started stamping my card over and over, filling up half the empty spots! As she was doing so, she said, "I don't know why I'm doing this. It just feels good!" I agreed that it felt pretty good to me, too, and we shared a laugh. As I turned to leave and put my hand on the door, a surge of adrenaline suddenly shot thru me. In that moment, I realized what had just happened. "All That and A Bag of Chips" had just revealed Itself to be very, very real indeed.

The "work," is not to be perfect, because perfect human beings don't exist. The work is to be perfectly *aware*. Aware that we are not alone, that there is a force eager to interact, play and be available to us. As we become more aware that we are surrounded by and are an integral part of a group of spiritual beings, that awareness allows us to bring something to the table in our exchange with them. Any efforts towards embracing our spiritual essence are rewarded. We become more conscious of the fact that we are part of this grand life, not just observers. We signed up for a soul expanding experience and we are going through it with a team of others who are depending on us to make it our best effort yet. They, in turn, are happy to demonstrate their appreciation of our efforts in both large and small ways.

As I've learned by studying many near-death experiences and accounts of life-between-life regressions, our Soul outlined Its major plan for this human incarnation before we were born. It communicates overall direction regularly with our SST. However we, as humans, have much leeway in the choices we can make. There are many, many junctures in your life where you are free to take a variety of different directions. But, the major lessons for your life are predestined. These include opportunities to hone certain skills such as compassion and forgiveness, which are carried over from previous lifetimes. Your Soul's plan for the experience of certain opportunities cannot be overridden. However, when you are successful in achieving certain developmental goals, such as spiritual courage or emotional intelligence, your basket of available fruits will increase. That is what is meant by "The fruits are the result of the work." I would take it further and say the fruits are contained within the work. That is because the very act of becoming conscious of and building a respect for your team automatically puts you in a position that is above common understanding. As you walk the earth aware that there is a powerful team which goes before you and follows behind keeping your back, you receive a gift of peace and security unlike any other. And always remember, there is no separation. You are a cherished and integral part of this team, which are cherished and integral parts of God.

Spiritual medium, James Van Praagh, has said he was in charge of soldiers directing people to kill others in several of his past lifetimes. Now he is experiencing the flip-side of that in helping spirits who have passed over to communicate with their loved ones. This awesome healing process has allowed him to experience both sides of the situation, which seems to be something our souls enjoy doing. Billy Fingers, through his sister Annie Kagan, penned a beautiful tell all about his experiences on the other side in the awesome book, The Afterlife of Billy Fingers. Billy was a bad-boy drug addict. After passing, one of the things he communicated to his sister from the other side was that his soul had *wanted* to experience what addiction was like in this lifetime. She has said that as a result, she doesn't judge

93

people negatively anymore. She's learned that our soul chooses to expand by experiencing both sides of many issues throughout many lifetimes.

This is why self-acceptance and self-forgiveness are so important. As long as we hold on to condemnation for things we or someone else did, we could be purchasing a ticket to a front row seat in a subsequent lifetime that gives us the experience of being on the receiving end of the same transgression. Our Soul, however, does not see things as punishments. The Soul would never punish itself. From the Soul's perspective, since there is no death only the infinite continuation of life, nothing is so heinous that it cannot be used for the expansion of wisdom, love and understanding. Experiencing both sides of situations facilitates the growth of wisdom through "having been there." You see, our Souls realize this life is just temporary. As such, they can pick out parts of any negative experience for promoting our growth. Every opportunity encountered by the Spirit (the part of the soul we are here on earth) is for the sake of experience. All experience serves to expand your Soul into a greater sense of compassion and understanding for self and for others. This process is necessary, because compassion is the heart of love and love is the essence of the Life Force.

As we've discussed, we are each a part of the body of God. God as the Source of All Life, never dies. It does, however, require continued experience in order to remain viable and alive. That's where we come in. We perform an incredible service in allowing the whole of creation to carry on by continuing to expand the energy of God through our earthly life experiences. That, my friends, is why we are seen by those in spirit as being so incredibly awesome. That is why, when we choose to create a conscious bond with our SST, a huge amount of assistance becomes available to us. We open the door for them to partner with us and they cherish the opportunity to participate in our lives..

You see, we are the rock stars of the universe and it does us well to remember that. And, to remember that our trials give us the opportunity to see situations from a larger perspective. I know it's incredibly difficult to understand while in the midst of any challenging situation. But it may help to remember that our Soul is after the experience of generating strength, power, compassion, forgiveness and understanding. When we can rise above the drama of our lives for a moment and gain that larger perspective, we can embrace the situation for what it is, an opportunity to participate in and to impart an experience for all of heaven to celebrate. We then open a channel for healing energy to flow to us. When we achieve the higher vibrations of strength, compassion, understanding, faith and the like, our Soul views it as a home-run. That win then opens the gate for the flow of energy that allows healing and solutions of all types to take place.

The intention to focus on healing the situation brings forth the energy which creates miracles. As previously discussed, our intention is an extremely powerful tool. It works to direct energy. Then releasing the problem, at least for awhile each day, allows your SST to do their job and sends a clear message of self-worth to your Soul. These are all necessary components in resolving any situation. And, remember, you are first and foremost a spiritual being having a temporary physical experience. Even if change is not immediately apparent in your earth life, much work is being done in the spiritual realm. NOTHING ever goes unnoticed or unrecorded. Your efforts to partner with your SST will always bear fruit.

We can make the most of our time here by focusing on our best experience from no matter where we happen to be. This is an action of self love. No matter how dire your circumstances appear, if you put forth some effort into relieving yourself from pain, that act of compassion towards yourself will be noted as another home-run. The universe always takes note of whatever work you do towards achieving your best life, even if it's to read a good book or go for a walk or do something for someone less fortunate so you'll stop focusing on your own problem. With practice, you will learn more and more how to honor your sacred self. And, by doing so, you will automatically attract more assistance from the group of spiritual beings imbued with supernatural powers who have the ability to assist you.

That said, remember, this is not heaven. On earth we have important work to do. Some of that work involves the mature acceptance of certain conditions. The practice of emotional maturity is one of the opportunities we were seeking by coming here, as it requires immense spiritual strength to achieve. Therefore, all our requests, will not be granted, period. Although he brought forth many miracles, Jesus could not save himself from being murdered, even though he prayed for it. In heaven all our requests are immediately answered and we are given what we ask for, except maybe a few things...which is our reason for coming here in the first place. We wanted to experience something we could not experience in heaven.

When my children were in middle school, they had to read a book called The Giver. It was about an advanced society which had effectively ended all war, aggression and other forms of negative behavior. By eliminating extreme emotion, they were able to exist in an exceptionally cooperative environment. They were able to focus all their mental energy in the pursuit of more civilized activities, such as logic and order. By eliminating passion, they effectively eliminated greed, envy, jealousy and a host of other negative emotions that lead to problematic behaviors.

They lived in a world of order and cooperation where no one was ever sad or miserable. Unfortunately, no one was ever truly ecstatic about anything either. They all just led very dispassionate and boring lives. They had evolved to a point where they could no longer even see in color or understand what art or music were. Theirs was a sterile, yet extremely efficient and peaceful way of life.

Now, I am not proposing that heaven operates this way, necessarily. The stories I've read by those who have passed over and returned to talk about it reveal a beautiful place of incredibly loving souls living together in a wonderfully cooperative environment. However, I do believe there are certain opportunities available to us here on earth that are not available to us in heaven. There had to be a compelling reason to come to earth in the first place. For us to want to incarnate in physical form into a world so relatively unevolved as to have many inhabitants still behaving like savages, killing and maiming each other, meant there must be something special here that we wanted to experience.

Our true nature, as part of the Omnipotent Divine God, is that we are extremely powerful beings ourselves. As I said before, we are part of the power we call God. Together, as part of the body of God, we created this world, just as it is. We created it for a very special purpose. Since we love ourselves as part of the Divine, we would not create something that was not a gift of love. This world, just the way it is, provides the perfect opportunity to grow and to expand the essence of love itself.

After all, It's not like we didn't know what we were getting ourselves into. We were not sent here as some type of punishment. God does not punish Itself. As divine beings, we are never punished, Quite to the contrary, we are given gifts. Along with the negative side of this world, and perhaps because of it, earth provides awesome opportunities to gain

98

emotional maturity and more. You see, these experiences are not available in heaven. In heaven, there is no need to generate compassion, because there is no misunderstanding or pain. There is no need to generate forgiveness, because no one hurts another. Because they are acutely aware of their oneness, everyone is already cooperative, supportive and loving. It makes complete sense, therefore, that we wanted to come to a world which gives us the glorious opportunity to practice generating these things.

Are you beginning to get the picture? I believe we had to develop an environment that would allow us to exercise our spiritual muscles, which is why I feel we collectively decided to create a world such as this. Like any strong athlete, we needed a place to come to every once in awhile where we could strengthen our ability to do what we were created to do. A world where we could practice being the fearless, powerful beings that we are. A world where we could love life under all conditions and experience ourselves as winners, even when our environment didn't support us. This world, just as it is, is the perfect environment for all that and more. In a world that is still so Neanderthal and backward in so many ways, we have a glorious opportunity to hone our skills as the awesome immortal spiritual beings we are.

Just like professional downhill skiers. Sure, hanging out in the lodge is great, but there comes a time when we need to go to the top of that mountain and do what we do best! Ski with complete abandon down that hill, flying with total trust in our own capabilities and in the team which surrounds us. We need to practice remembering our team is with us under all circumstances and live our lives with absolutely no fear of abandonment. As we vow to never ever abandon ourselves to fear or hopelessness, we offer up yet another win to the universe, which is forever cheering us on.

Chapter 11
Sorry, No

Many years ago, I began dating a man who I felt fit my ideal vision of a perfect partner. He liked to do the same things I liked to do, enjoyed traveling, had a great job and was also somewhat playful, like me. After dating for a couple of months, I fell totally in love with him and began entertaining visions of a house with a white picket fence, 2.5 children and living happily ever after. In total, we dated for about a year. But, during that time something wasn't exactly right. Occasionally, he would disappear for a couple weeks. Then he'd do something really sweet to win me back. It bears mentioning that back then I suffered from an extremely low self-esteem and put up with things I would never put up with now. Deep down, I thought I didn't deserve to be loved. This erroneous belief manifested itself in my intimate relationships. Whatever the situation and no matter how disrespectfully I was being treated, I stubbornly stuck with my desire to have a permanent relationship with him.

Then about eight months into our courtship, my father died unexpectedly. I was having a hard time sleeping as a result, so I went to see a psychologist in order to get some help with my insomnia. It's interesting looking back, and I never told anyone at the time, but I couldn't sleep because I often had a strong feeling my father was in the room with me.

Because I didn't understand the immense affection our loved ones in spirit have for us, this feeling of my dad's nearness made me feel extremely uneasy.

After a couple visits with the psychologist, he asked to talk to Ryan to find out if there was anything he, as my boyfriend, could do to support me. I suspect he also felt my tenuous relationship with Ryan was unhealthy for me and likely contributing to my feelings of fear. I remember during this shared visit with the psychologist, trying in vain to suppress an incredible urge I had to go to the bathroom. But, eventually my bladder won out and I was forced to excuse myself from the room. During the time I was gone, the psychologist and Ryan spoke among themselves. When I returned the psychologist seemed to be trying to get Ryan to admit something. He said, "You're trying to protect Adriana, aren't you?" I remember thinking, "Protect me from what?" Ryan said nothing. At my next solo visit, the psychologist told me it was obvious from his chat with Ryan that he had an "alternate agenda." I wasn't sure what he meant by that comment and, unwisely, didn't ask.

Ryan ended the relationship a few days later. This all occurred around two weeks after my father had died and, coincidentally, around the same time the 1989 earthquake hit my area further adding to my feelings of devastation and bewilderment. Needless to say, I was distraught and didn't understand why my relationship had to end. I had done everything I could to try and be the "perfect girlfriend." We

102

never really disagreed and I couldn't understand why he didn't want to be with me. I knew his previous girlfriend was still contacting him occasionally, but she had moved back east and I thought he was over her. And, although Ryan was a staunch Catholic, I had been more than willing to give up my open spirituality in favor of having a permanent relationship with him.

I was beside myself with grief over the termination of our relationship. That coupled with my dad's death, sent me into a state-of-mind where I no longer trusted men. As a result, for the next six years from age 32 to 38, I had no romantic relationships. The pain at having lost Ryan, who I loved so much, and my father at the same time was overwhelming. This was not a conscious choice, but it seemed men just stayed away from me. This demonstrates how strong our subconscious can be at either attracting or repelling people and situations.

My career, however, excelled. But, I still longed to have children and a family. I remember making the decision that if I still hadn't met anyone who I felt was marriage material by the time I was 40, I would adopt. I even began making phone calls to orphanages in Mexico. The Directors there told me it is very rare for a child to have permanent residence in a Mexican orphanage, because family members almost always surface to take the child home. They further explained that when there is a situation where adoption is the only option, they always give preferential treatment to local

Mexican families first. This was disappointing, but understandable. However, I still wanted to have my own family and was eventually blessed to finally meet someone who felt the same way. This was over 20 years ago and I now have three awesome children.

A few months ago, I was visiting my profile on LinkedIn.com, the professional career website. I had joined a sub-group within Linkedin and guess whose profile popped up as a possible ex-colleague? As Ryan's smiling mug stared back at me from the screen, I knew I could never request making a "connection" with him nor did I want to. However, I couldn't help but be curious regarding his life and how things had turned out for him.

My experience in recruiting and performing background checks as a Human Resource Manager kicked in. A few minutes and several keystrokes later, I had my answer. Ryan had married a woman in 1995, not sure if it was the ex-girlfriend. She seemed to have come from a wealthy Texan family. Given his somewhat uppity nature, this was something Ryan would definitely appreciate. She was into horses. Given his somewhat wimpy nature, this was something Ryan would likely hate. They had never purchased a house, but instead bought a condo in a snobby Silicon Valley suburb, something Ryan would have loved. She eventually left him and they divorced. Hummm. Pictures on her Facebook page revealed she'd bought herself a beautiful ranch in the southern part of the county following the divorce and now boards horses. Her status listed her as being in a new relationship. But, most importantly, they never had any children.

I suddenly realized that could have been me! However, since I'm allergic to horses, I wouldn't even have that to enjoy! My marriage would have fallen apart, I would not have had any children and I would be completely alone at 50-something. That was obviously not what God had in store for my life. As a result, I no longer question when the answer to my prayers is "No." Because even in the no, there is a big yes, if you just trust your team.

There are times when we might feel in conflict with our Soul's intention, especially when we don't feel we are getting what we want. But, we need to bear in mind that our Soul knows what it is doing. As I said before, our Soul (our larger spiritual self, which is always one with God) came here to experience certain things. Hence, our sojourn into this physicality for the purpose of exercising our spiritual muscles in areas where they needed a workout. Patience may be one of those areas needing exercise, faith without truly knowing - another. Learning to love ourselves when it seems no one else does is invaluable at building our self-esteem. And self-esteem is another form of honoring the Light of God within ourselves. It allows the light to shine brighter. And the brighter the Light of God shines within you, the stronger and healthier cell within the body of God you will be.

Don't forget that our Soul has a larger perspective from the other side regarding the things we wished to experience before we came here. And it never loses that perspective. Our time here is limited and the Soul knows that in order to achieve everything we wanted to experience, certain situations must be allowed to exist. So, no, we won't necessarily get everything we want, and that is by design. That said, never forget that your Soul loves you beyond measure. The service you are performing for yourself and the entire universe by coming here is extremely appreciated.

There is an awesome book called Where Angels Walk by Joan Wester Anderson. In it she shares numerous powerful angelic encounters. I was discussing the book with my friend Kate, who just happened to buy that same book on the same day I bought my copy. This wouldn't have seemed so odd, except that the book was written 24 years ago and we both made the purchase on the same day while attending swap meets in towns 2,000 miles apart. That being the case, I felt I should pay particular attention to the information that book had to offer. We were discussing the incidents of angelic interventions outlined in it and I realized many of these occurred in the midst of heroic feats of courage. It occurred to me that our Spiritual Support Team seems to be especially active whenever we demonstrate courage, whenever we venture out of our comfort zone, whenever we do something that requires a bit of moxie or guts on our part. In those times it's as if we are bringing more confidence to the table in our relationship with our team and it definitely gets their attention. What we are bringing is strength, faith, and most importantly, trust. In those times, especially, you can be sure their presence is fierce. Like the "trust game" where one person trusts the other enough to fall backwards into their outstretched arms, I believe our trust is met with an equal measure of our team's powerful support.

Courage comes in many forms. It may come in the form of accepting that someone may not want to be with you, of forgiving a huge transgression, of walking off a job, or standing up for what you believe even if you might lose some friends. These are examples of a few situations I've been in where my SST made their presence extremely well known by providing me with incredible support. It makes sense that courage, in its many forms, calls them forth with an immense drawing power. I believe the demonstration of courage is one of the main reasons we came into physical form. Did you get that? The opportunity to experience courage is not available to you anywhere else to the degree that it is available on this earth. Whenever you are demonstrating courage, while trusting your SST to surround you, you can be sure they will be there with swords drawn and miracle bags at the ready. I have seen it time and time again.

Chapter 12

The Recorder

It has been demonstrated to me repeatedly and beyond a shadow of a doubt, that there is much more happening in this life than meets the eye. The fact that we have a powerful group of evolved beings, our Spiritual Support Team, who constantly surround us is proof that there is a greater power at work here. They are made up of God, the Light, the Creator of all there is, together with friends and relatives who love us who have passed on and now reside in the light and our special posse of additional spiritual guardians and protectors. This holy group is available to provide encouragement, support and can work miracles. The reason why they are able to work what we view as miracles, is because they are 1) unfettered by form, so time and particulate matter are non-issues for them, 2) they have a broader view of things, so possess a greater perspective regarding what's going on, and 3) from where they reside, they are closer to the Light. This proximity allows them to be acutely aware of the fact that they are individual aspects of the Light. They understand that the Light of God shines through them. They are, therefore, easily able to serve as powerful focusers of that Light. They are aspects of the Divine, just as we are, but they are more acutely aware of and closely connected to it.

The experiences I've shared in this book are just a few I've had which bear witness to these facts. This Spiritual Support Team is not just available to a few, they are available to everyone. Many people have experienced even greater miracles than I have. It is my understanding that anyone who puts forth an effort into developing a pure and trusting relationship and open communication with their SST will be rewarded with irrefutable evidence of their presence.

The fact that there is something very powerful going on around us which we cannot see is by design. Because perhaps if we could see them, we'd know the incredible assistance that is available to us and the difficulties of this world would lose some of their challenge. The trials and tribulations of our earthly condition would no longer afford us the opportunity to strengthen ourselves the way we intended them to by coming here. We'd no longer hold on to the illusion that we are alone.

However, there comes a time in the evolution of any society where certain truths must reveal themselves in order for that civilization to progress forward. I see it happening on our earth plane now. Ever ready digital cameras often capture incidents that seem other-worldly in nature and defy explanation. Asian practitioners of Qi-Gong and other medicineless modalities are performing healing miracles, like shrinking tumors, that are captured on ultrasound cameras as they occur. Children who can remember past lives in detail are being recorded and their stories investigated, oftentimes revealing amazing accuracy. Numerous individuals, including noted physicians, are having near-death experiences and returning to tell their amazing stories. Paranormal sightings are becoming commonplace, where reports of strangers appearing at just the right moment to provide assistance and then disappearing without a trace are happening with greater frequency. The new ease of shooting videos and the technology in the speed of digital photography allows images which vibrate at a higher frequency to be captured with greater clarity than ever before. Added to that, social media provides a platform for sharing information and photographs quickly to the masses, which was not previously available. So, although I believe these things have always occurred, it is now easier for them to be recorded and disseminated.

I've heard that, when you begin to believe they are possible, you will see things you couldn't see before. But, I always thought it was a theory that pertained only to relationships, money or fancy cars. Now I know it's true. Changing our beliefs about what is possible, rips a hole in the ceiling of a narrow reality. The spiritual adage, you'll see it when you believe it, is definitely true. Such was the case for me on the evening of June 30, 2015.

A few years ago, I'd begun reading some of Doreen Virtue's books and loved the way she never questions the reality of angels, but rather works at incorporating them into her everyday life. I can't remember when, but at some point I started reading information about life after death. I'd always

111

been interested in the topic, but since the miracle of finding my family occurred, I was now even more interested in the power of those in spirit. My daughter and I had also started watching old shows like the Ghost Whisperer, just for fun. Then the opportunity to see James Van Praagh, the show's executive producer, in my favorite beach town of Carmel presented itself. When nothing short of a miracle occurred to get us there, I knew there was something encouraging me to go down this learning path. We were able to get an awesome hotel room with a fireplace, full ocean view and tickets with lightening speed and ease. My daughter and I went to the event and had a wonderful time. I loved the way James was able to prove the existence of life after death by performing readings on people in the audience with incredible accuracy. I'd taken a course from Doreen Virtue in becoming a Certified Angel Card Reader several years before, and as a result of the weekend in Carmel, I decided I was going to learn how to incorporate messages from those who had passed on into my angel readings.

So I amped up my learning curve on life after death information. I devoured everything I could get my hands on, becoming one of Amazon's best customers on the subject. I had always enjoyed listening to true stories about near death experiences, which are about people who have died for a short while and then return to tell about their experience. Now, information in the form of books, videos and even personal accounts from friends and neighbors began pouring in.

Within a few months, I began to perform mediumship readings for family members whose relatives had passed on. To my surprise, the information that came through in those readings was incredibly accurate! For instance, in a reading with my cousin's wife, a vision of her mother appeared sitting on a couch knitting, occasionally rolling her eyes as she spoke. Although I had never met her mother, she said, "Yes, that's my mom!" Her mother communicated many things to me, including the message, "Drink more water." Interestingly, the next day my cousin's husband wasn't feeling well and went to see the doctor. Immediately upon examining him, the doctor said he was extremely dehydrated and ordered him to start drinking more water immediately or he would have to be admitted into the hospital.

I also had a phone reading with another 'new' cousin who had recently lost her young son. I'd never had the opportunity to meet him before he died. Through me he told her to "put away all the red items in my room." She gasped and said that's exactly what she was doing at that very moment! She said she was sitting in his room putting away the Los Angeles Angels sports memorabilia he had collected. She said, "Of course, you know the Angel's team colors." Not being a sports fan, nor from Southern California, I had no clue. She said "Red! It's red. And his room was filled with it." His spirit then asked me to tell to her to open the curtains to let more light in. She said, "He always wanted the curtains opened. He would go around the whole house opening them up." He also told me he was now with a man by the name of Anthony Padilla. Forgetting I was new to the family, she replied, "Oh, you knew him, Tony Padilla, right? He was Branden's grandfather." I said no, I had never met nor heard of him, but that she could rest assured that her son was with him, being taught in healing modalities and that they were both doing extremely well on the other side.

A final message came through in that reading from my young cousin regarding the name Matt. His spirit asked me to tell her to "Let Matt help." It turned out Matt was his best friend. She explained that Matt still comes around often offering to do things for the family.

In another reading for, Pearl, longtime girlfriend of Archie, she seemed shaken when she answered my phone call at our scheduled appointment time. She said, "You'll never guess what just happened! Right before you called, my cell phone rang. The Caller ID said it was Archie. But when I answered it, there was no one there!" Both Pearl & I knew his sister was now in possession of his cell phone. The thing was, the line had been disconnected the day before. Since his "call" came in right before mine, it was clear to both of us that Archie was anxious to talk with her.

Shortly after this, I decided I wanted to try doing readings for an on-line service. However, I didn't like the fact that they made clients pay for every minute of the reading. It

114

didn't feel right to have to rush through a reading while being so concerned with the clock. I don't think our friends in spirit like being rushed either. So, I gave up on that idea. However, the training I'd done had expanded my belief system in an undeniable way. I now KNEW beyond a shadow of a doubt our loved ones in spirit can communicate with us and that they are anxious to do so. This experience proved to me that there is continuity of life. We do not disappear when we die. We remain available to assist and communicate with our loved ones. I'd suspected it all along, but this was further proof. And, as you've probably guessed by now, I love proof.

When we work at expanding our belief systems, it opens up a whole new world of possibilities for us. When people still believed the world was flat, their belief in what was possible was limited to that understanding. What we currently know about the world of spirit is similar to what people knew about earth when they believed it to be flat. Embracing any new belief causes a paradigm shift in what we previously believed to be possible. It rips a hole in the ceiling of what we previously thought to be fact, to reveal an entire new level of reality. This is why I feel it's important to continue learning, especially if something is important to us. And, like I said, I've always wanted to know what we were doing here. Well, I was about to find out.

On the evening of June 30, 2015 just as I was awakening from a short nap I saw something that would change my life FOREVER. Around 5 p.m., shortly after returning from vacation with my family and being particularly tired, I uncharacteristically dozed off for a few minutes on the couch while watching television. My husband was sitting next to me deeply engrossed in one of his scientific journals.

In the very moment I was waking up, I clearly saw a young man appearing to be in his early thirties, descending the stairs, which are about 18 feet away from the couch where I was laying. He carried what looked to be a white notepad in his right arm and seemed to be engrossed in reading it as he gingerly bounded down my stairs! I am not sure if the notepad was an electronic one or a pad of paper, but it was clearly a notepad of some type.

I am typing this from notes I took later that same day. However, like most who have seen such beings, every detail of this moment is still firmly etched in my mind. As I was opening my eyes, my gaze went from his feet upwards. He was barefoot and had a tanned body. As my shocked eyes scanned upwards, I could even make out the blond hair on his legs! It appeared he had very light brown or dirty blond hair. I didn't get a good look at his face, as his head was bent down reading the notepad he was holding, but he was wearing a light blue t-shirt and tan shorts. I immediately recognized him as a ghost, if you will…a non-physical interloper for lack of a better word. In any case, I immediately raised my arm, pointed at him and shouted "You!"

Both my arm and voice felt a bit thick from sleep, but I was loud enough for both he and my husband to clearly hear me. In the moment he realized I could see him, he immediately did a 180 degree about-face and quickly headed back up the stairs. My husband who was sitting next to me heard me yell and looked up towards me first. His gaze followed my arm in the direction of my pointing finger. But, by the time he did so, the young man had disappeared back up the stairs. From where I was laying on the couch, you can only see the bottom three stairs. He was on the bottom step when he turned around and headed back up, so he quickly disappeared behind the wall where he could no longer be seen.

Heart beating fast and more than wide awake now, I exclaimed to my husband, "Did you see that?!" My husband seemed somewhat confused and shook his head. I quickly described what I had seen, then I got up and went to the stairs and looked up. Something inside me told me I would no longer be able to see him and I was right. Not that he was gone but, I surmised, now that I was fully awake my ability to see him was no longer functioning. I felt a strange realization come over me. The realization slowly washed over me that when we are "awake" in this world, we are actually asleep. We are unable to see what is going on right under our noses in the spiritual dimension that exists right here within our own world.

About a week after this incident, I had two more visions of spirits, both right upon awakening from a nap. However, both were considerably shorter. One occurred while watching the same television novella set in the 1800s that had been on TV when my initial visitor came down the stairs. This time I was also laying on the couch. As I opened my eyes, there about 3 feet away from me, standing to the right of my head, stood a small woman fully dressed in a period costume. Her dress, an off-white shade with a small black print, even had a bustle! She stood quietly to my right side intently watching the drama unfold on the television set in front of her. I purposely turned my head away while blinking myself completely awake, because I really wasn't interested in seeing any more spirits. However, a few nights later, while lying on the same couch under the same drowsy conditions, I briefly caught a glimpse of a man sitting at a desk in the corner of our living room! He was engrossed in working on something. The green lamp on his desk was clearly visible and he wore some type of visor on his head. But, this time unlike the others, the vision was opaque. Meaning I could see through his desk and view my own living room furniture on the other side. Again, after blinking myself completely awake, my ability to see him disappeared. Although these two instances of being able to see spirits who dwell among us was interesting, neither was as significant as the young man I had seen coming down the stairs a few days earlier.

I kept thinking about him and still had so many questions. Seeing him moving around, actually "working" in my home fascinated me. My first question was, what was he doing with that tablet? When I saw him, he seemed completely engrossed in reading whatever was written on it. When I looked at him, I got the distinct impression he was reviewing his own notes about something that he himself had written, perhaps something that had been going on in our house?

Another thing that struck me was the familiarity and ease with which he moved through my house. He was coming down the stairs rather swiftly, just like my kids do. I got the impression he spends a lot of time in our home. This tells me there is something going on with us humans that is of extreme interest to these beings who move around in our world. Without a doubt, they are observing and gathering information. And, without a doubt, they do not wish to be seen.

I suddenly realized EVERYTHING we do is being recorded. There is not one moment when we think we are alone, that we actually are. Obviously, that is by design. Because what people do when they think nobody is watching is much more revealing than what is done in the presence of others.

Also of interest were the clothes he was wearing. A light blue t-shirt and tan shorts that *exactly* resembled a pair my husband owns. After the incident, I went to my husband's dresser drawer where those clothes are normally kept. There they were, still neatly folded the way they had been before. But, I remember so clearly seeing the orange detail around the zipper and button on those tan shorts as the young man descended our stairs. They were either the same exact clothes or an incredibly accurate copy. The young man was about as tall, but in somewhat better shape than my husband, I could see his abs through the t-shirt. But he wore the shirt the same way my husband does...tucked in at the waist. I wondered if he was dressed in my husband's clothes in an effort to look like him in case he was spotted?

For the next few weeks I could think of little else other than what I had seen. I carried an odd sense of fear mixed with exhilaration, a strange anticipation that I might walk into a room and see someone standing there. I prayed that whatever Beings surround me ALWAYS be of the Light. That helped ease my trepidation somewhat. My husband, who is extremely unemotional, asked me what I was afraid of? He felt I should make an effort to talk to the young man. But, I wasn't that brave. If the young man, (or any other spirits) chose to reveal themselves to me again, I would welcome them. But I wasn't going to actively open that door again. The fact is that, while I loved hearing the voices of my Spiritual Team Members when they'd prayed over me that day in church so many years ago, actually *seeing* them now had left me a bit shaken. By the same token, I was *thrilled* that I'd been given the experience and felt immensely blessed to have witnessed that young man with the writing tablet in my house.

Bob Olson, host of AfterlifeTV, once discussed having a life between life regression during which he discovered his "job" on the other-side was being a teacher. He said he specifically taught about fear. It makes sense that souls who reside in the non-physical dimension require teachings about things we humans encounter here on earth, as their environment does not lend itself to those types of experiences. Perhaps after we've returned to the non-physical and been there for a while, we begin to forget about certain "human conditions" and need refresher courses before planning a new incarnation. In any case, I began wondering if my visitor was a teacher or teacher's assistant whose purpose was to gather information for educational purposes. A few weeks later, as I was sharing my story with the folks on Emanuel Swedeborg's site, they suggested the young man may have been an "angel-in-training" which would explain why he might not have sufficiently cloaked himself to keep from being seen.

For several months following this incident I believed I was an anomaly at having been able to see what I did. However, I was soon to learn I am not the only one who has had such ghostly encounters. As I was planning an overnight trip to Jamestown, I read some reviews on Trip Advisor about the Jamestown Historic Hotel built in 1859. I repeatedly saw mention of a ghost which is reported to inhabit the hotel. I had never before read a first hand account of a ghost sighting, but right there on Trip Advisor was a posting from a gentleman dated October 26, 2015 who goes by the name Seniortravelalot. After raving about the rooms and the food, he also wrote this about his stay at the hotel: *"I would be remiss if I didn't mention a ghost sighting. At 3:44 a.m. I heard a noise in our room and woke up. Next to the window I spied a quiet, dark haired young lady standing under what appeared to be a spotlight. She seemed to have a book in her hand. This sighting (almost like a hologram) lasted only three-four seconds! I quickly fell back asleep, but in the morning looked for the light source she had been standing under. There was none. It was only later that I learned about other reports of a friendly ghost. For me, I could only assume that it was the result of that last glass of Port that the owner offered me!"*

Well, as for me, I had not been drinking anything, so I know beyond a shadow of a doubt what I saw and that it was very real. It's interesting that Seniortravelalot's experience was similar to mine in that he was able to see the spirit immediately upon awakening and only for a few moments.

I've heard that when our brains are in a highly meditative (or alpha) state, such as they are immediately upon awakening, we are actually much more open to what happening in other dimensions. Apparently, toddler's brains are often on this frequency, which explains how they sometimes report being able to see their spiritual visitors quite clearly.

I was very happy to read about Seniortravelalot's sighting, because it helped me realize that I was not crazy. As I began sharing this story, friends and relatives started telling me stories of their own or their children's angelic sightings. I started to realize there are many more people in this world who have experienced these types of sightings, but who are reluctant to come forward for fear of being labeled. I was happy to learn that such sightings are not completely unheard of and it excites me to learn more from others who have had them. I started wondering if the hotel's spirit, who carries a book as well, is herself also working as a recorder.

Following are more notes (in italics) written the day after the sighting in my home on June 30, 2015.

Now, a couple days later, not being able to erase the event from my mind, I have begun to ponder some significant questions. What if there isn't actually a "heaven," but rather various levels of physicality? What if what prophets, seers and children have reported seeing have in actuality just been beings

*from other worlds, or dimensions, which vibrate at a
higher frequency than ours? And, if so, what
difference does it make? To us, they are still "spiritual"
beings.*

*They appear to be more advanced than us in certain
ways. The young man obviously knew how to remain
"cloaked" to keep from being seen by physical eyes.
That isn't a simple trick. So, obviously they can see
us, know all our behaviors, habits, comings and
goings. The implications of this are huge. Do they ride
in the car with us? Obviously so. Can we invite them
to go places with us? I'm sure we can. Why are they
so interested in us? Why don't they want to be seen?
Why did he go to such elaborate measures to "blend
in" by wearing exact replicas of my husband's clothes?*

*I wonder if maybe we're more "advanced" than they
are in other ways. Or, perhaps because of our limited
finite perspective, we're able to experience things in a
way that they cannot....and it fascinates them.*
Remember the story, The Giver, where an "advanced"
society had evolved to no war, no negativity, just
complete cooperation, but in the process had lost the
capacity to experience all negative emotion? *I wonder
if my visitor comes from such a world? A dimension
without anger or hate, but also where the opportunity*

for compassion and forgiveness cannot present itself as a result? Do they observe us in order to learn more about these things from our experiences? Do we provide them the opportunity to somehow experience these things vicariously through us?

I'm still very curious as to what and why was he "recording" and for what reason? And, to whom he was reporting.

In thinking about what was going on in our home at that time, I realize that for the previous couple days and into that morning, my daughter and I had been experiencing some very emotionally charged issues that involved a lot of compassion, understanding and forgiveness on both our parts. I'm wondering if that situation was of particular interest to them. The situation that my daughter and I were going through was extremely similar to something my father and I had gone through when he was still alive. I had behaved with my dad similarly to the way my daughter was behaving towards me. Earlier that day, I had stood in the bathroom upstairs and "told my dad" I now understood how I had made him feel by my behavior so many years ago and offered him my heartfelt compassion and forgiveness. Was that incident of forgiveness what had summoned my visitor?

To elaborate, a couple days before this incident, we had been on vacation in a small cabin in the mountains. It was just my husband, me and our twins, then age 14. Our older son had decided to stay home. My daughter and I are very close and typically share almost everything. The cabin we were staying in was quite small with only one bathroom. The final evening of our stay, my daughter and I were in the bathroom at the same time. I offhandedly began telling her about a problem I was having with my husband, her father. I don't recall exactly what the details were, but my husband can be 'challenging' at times and I often shared my frustrations with her. This time she looked at me and said, in no uncertain terms, "Mom, I don't want to hear about this!" She went on to tell me that whatever my issue was, it made her uncomfortable and she wanted me to stop talking about it.

The bluntness of her comment felt like a cold slap across my face. Of course, she was absolutely right! But it still hurt me to hear her say it. I felt like my best friend had just slammed a door on me. I know I was being emotionally immature, but the hurt I felt was overwhelming. My daughter and I had always been able to speak about everything and we had often been one another's support throughout life's ups and downs. To hear her now tell me she basically felt abused by my oversharing hurt, no matter how inappropriate I had been. Somewhat embarrassed, I immediately apologized and told her I would never speak about that type of thing in her presence again and left the room.

The next day on the three-hour drive home, I felt distraught. I just kept thinking about my dad. You see, my father used to do the exact same thing to me. After I left home I would often make the three hour drive to visit him, coincidentally to the town we had just been vacationing in. I loved my dad very much and he loved me, too. However, for as long as I can remember, he would come into my room, close the door and start to complain about my mother. Finally one day, after hearing him say he was going to leave her for the hundredth time, I told him I didn't want to hear about it anymore. I told him if he wasn't going to do anything about his personal situation, then he should keep the details to himself. What I was trying to communicate, but failed miserably at doing, was that it made me sad to see him so unhappy. I will never forget the look of hurt and betrayal in his eyes as my blunt comment struck him. I had obviously hurt him very deeply.

The way my father handled his hurt was to write me out of his will. Actually, he made sure not leave a will or family trust at all, after having assured me repeatedly for years that he would. I was angry, not because of the money, but because of an unkept promise. My dad was the most important person in my life, but he had a habit of not keeping promises sometimes. So when he died, it was my turn to feel the sting of his betrayal. Even though we were incredibly close and I loved him very much, I didn't cry at his funeral. I'm an extremely sensitive person, but my heart was numb. Looking back, I realize it was actually a gift. Because if I hadn't been angry with my dad when he died, I would have been completely devastated. Devastated to the point of probably not being able to function, because at the time he was the only family I had.

So, going back to the incident with my daughter. Yes, the hurt was huge for me, just like I now realized it had been for my dad. That's when I had a conversation in my bedroom with my dad's spirit. I told him I now understood how I had hurt him and that I was very, very sorry. I then went to my daughter's room and asked her to sit down. I told her that she was right in that certain things should not be shared by adults with children. I explained that I had always been there for her and wanted her to know that even though what she had said had hurt, I would always continue to be there for her. I took the opportunity to remind her that when she complains about her brothers, I always listen and offer support and encouragement to her. I told her that I wanted to make sure she knew I would always be there for her no matter what and that I appreciated her being there for me, as well. In her emotionally mature way, my daughter told me she wanted that too. But she again reiterated that she did not want to hear about any issues I had with her father and that if I needed support I should seek it from my girlfriends.

Although I was a bit shocked at her candidness, I agreed and told her - in a loving way - that I now realized how my own dad had felt when I'd told him the same thing so many years ago. I thanked her and told her that all this had helped me to understand his perspective better. I told her she had actually helped me to forgive him. It was a moment of extreme compassion and understanding. We both hugged and I left the room.

It was just a few hours later that the incident occurred where I fell asleep on the couch to be awakened by the sight of my visitor gingerly descending my staircase with his notebook in hand.

More of my notes from the day after the incident follow in italics:

> *My daughter was still upstairs watching a movie on her Kindle when he descended the stairs. Although my husband was sitting next to me on the couch, by the time he looked up, our visitor had disappeared. I now believe my heavenly visitor is a recorder of sorts, working on behalf of the Light, the collective wisdom of all souls.*

In her book, Application of Impossible Things, when Natalie Sudman had her near-death experience and arrived on the other side, she found herself in a gathering of

129

thousands of souls. These personalities, besides offering incredible admiration, performed a type "download of information" on her from her experiences on earth. What I gather from this is that thousands of Beings on the other side benefit from our experiences here on earth, as it adds to their own knowledge-base. More of my notes:

It occurred to me that since my visitor was coming from upstairs where my daughter was in her room, he may have been downloading information from her regarding our interaction. When I went up to her room a few minutes later, she was peacefully laying on her bed like usual, watching her Kindle. However, I know that energy tends to remain in a space long after an occurrence, especially when there has been strong emotion involved.

It is only through direct experience that wisdom can be achieved. I believe we came to earth in order to provide that direct experience. That experience provides the wisdom through which the universe grows. It is through us that the wisdom of that which we call God, continues to expand. It is important to realize that this Source is alive. As a living organism It must continue to expand, or it will contract. That is because anything living is in constant motion - or change - either one way or the other. As the parts of God who come to earth and take human form, we are chartered with providing the direct experience by which God's wisdom and knowledge-base grows. If we did not volunteer to do this, existence itself would eventually terminate.

That is why all the accounts I've read from those who re-enter the non-physical dimension describe being greeted by loving Beings who display an immense amount of appreciation. They repeatedly report receiving the impression that these Beings consider us to be "very cool." I believe we are held in incredibly high esteem for having the courage to venture into physicality in the first place. This finite physical form is not our natural environment. It takes courage and an immense determination for us as spiritual beings to focus our energy into corporal bodies and to stay here for a lifetime. Our experience in this world, just as it is, adds immensely to the overall wisdom of Universal Intelligence.

This explains why we are always being monitored and recorded, especially when it comes to incidents involving courage, compassion, understanding, boundary setting, conflict resolution, and a host of other soul expanding activities.

Perhaps that is why when I was in the first grade, at a new school and away from everything that was familiar to me, I experienced being watched by spiritual beings with such extreme interest. They obviously wanted to see how I handled my new situation, which required a considerable amount of bravery on my part.

Natalie Sudman describes their admiration for us as stemming from the immense amount of energy we expend in being able to remain "focused in physicality", which apparently is no small feat. I can't help but wonder if they are as impressed by us as we are by them.

> *Another item of note is that my visitor seemed very comfortable in his surroundings. He was gingerly bounding down the stairs, as if he did so on a regular basis. He was also barefoot, which is interesting. Most visitors to our home know we all typically leave our shoes at the front door. Was it a sign of respect for my wishes? Also very interesting is that the tan colored shorts and light blue t-shirt he was wearing looked EXACTLY like ones my husband owns. Was he actually wearing them? Or had he made a copy and donned them? What is it that is so powerful that can do that?*

Good question. What is it that is so powerful!? As has been demonstrated by the many experiences of miracles I've had in my life, our spiritual team members have incredible power over this physical world. That is because they have been anointed by God to assist in perpetuating Infinity, which is no small task. Since this finite world and its associated limitations exist for the Soul's experiential purposes, it stands to reason that those who remain in spirit are unencumbered by our physical limitations. That is why time, matter, circumstances and earthly conditions hold no power over their capabilities.

What is so powerful that it can shape-shift, copy, and appear to be wearing material items? What is so powerful it can reach into the future and backwards into the past to affect outcomes, such as many of the divine interventions I've experienced? Well, I'd guess the same anointed energies which are sparks of the Divine Itself. These sparks are capable of drawing energy from Source to answer prayer.

God is not a myth, like some think, but rather the Life Force Itself. And, although we are all a part of this Life Force, the difference between us and the Spiritual Beings who are imbued with supernatural power is that they are aware of their special place in the Body of God and we, for the most part, are not. But, obviously, that is by design as well. For, if we were so consciously entangled with Source as they are, we would not struggle with our everyday mortal challenges. If we didn't struggle with trust, we wouldn't need to reach for faith. And, it is our struggling which creates the "rub" the universe needs to grow.

No matter what our current state, I know that one day we all return to embrace the reality of our spiritual grandeur. Until then, I'm not sure about you, but the members of my Spiritual Support Team are definitely Beings with whom I wish to partner. These are Beings whose energy I want to invite to be stronger in my life. And, like anything that becomes stronger for us, I know I can do that by focusing on the fact that they exist and are available to me everyday in every situation, no matter how challenging.

He also appeared very solid. Not opaque, ghostly or filmy in any way, but completely solid in form. Nor was he floating. His feet were definitely touching the stairs as he descended. This raises other questions, such as are these highly vibrating beings affected by gravity?

We could assume he was doing these things - walking, appearing in form, etc. for my benefit. However, the fact that he seemed completely surprised by my ability to see him indicates otherwise.

Interestingly, a couple weeks after this incident I found the shorts my angelic visitor was wearing now had a huge rip in them. The long tear ran vertically up one leg. My husband had absolutely no idea how that rip had occurred. The shorts were now unwearable, so I placed them on top of the washing machine, planning to save them. However, they disappeared from there and I have never again been able to find them again. I wonder if, having been discovered as touched by other-worldly forces, those shorts had to disappear.

After these incidents, I had a brain CT performed due to occasional headaches I'd started having. I secretly feared I might have a brain tumor, which would explain the visions.

However, my brain scan (performed on 9/7/16) came back completely normal, having turned out to be a lack of sleep due to my teenager working odd hours and waking me up in the middle of the night when he gets home. Therefore, any physiological causes for the visions on my part can be ruled out.

More than a year has passed since I saw my angelic visitors. Part of me misses being able to see them, but I know they are here. If they are with me, they are with you as well. They are present in your home. They walk around in our world. They record and report our behavior...even when we are alone and think nobody is watching. God is always watching through them. They are non-judgmental, they are God's angels and they are with us - always. They move freely among us here on earth. I am convinced they come here for purposes of observing and reporting in order to learn from our human condition. And the service we provide of allowing them to observe our mortal experience, does not go without appreciation.

When we focus on their presence and remain aware of their existence, just like a friend who thinks of you often, they are drawn to participate more actively in our lives. I challenge you to expand your current understanding. Become aware of the spiritual support group that surrounds you, whether you can see them or not. When you do so, you will begin to see daily evidence of their love for you. Remain vigilant. Remain thankful. The incidents of joy you will experience as a result will not fail to amaze you.

Chapter 13
The Revelation

My friend Kate meditates. Unlike myself, she meditates a lot and is quite persistent about it. After meditating regularly for several months, something awesome happened and she caught it on video. She didn't just catch it once, but many, many times. The same thing happened recently with another friend of mine, Amy, who is a medium. Both ladies had first noticed their cats acting strangely. Yes, I know it sounds cliché, but stick with me. It was as if their cat's eyes were following something in the room which neither woman could see. So, as is the custom these days, they immediately grabbed their cell phones and pressed record on the camera. When they played back the movies, they saw something incredible. There, clearly on the screen, were numerous light emitting orbs flying all around the room. Some moved quickly, others more slowly. Some were larger and denser than others. Some were clear, others filmy, some were colored. All, however, were glowing. Since then, both my friends have taken many, many movies of these light emitting flying orbs. They've shared some with me which you can view on my website at www.revadriana.com.

Some may be tempted, as I was at first, to dismiss these energy emitting flying orbs which can sometimes be recorded on camera, as dust or some other particulate matter.

However, after recording them for a while, something incredible happened. This was witnessed by several people, even my scientifically oriented husband for one. After witnessing the phenomenon himself, my husband explains it this way, "These orbs are vibrating at a frequency of light that is just outside our range of vision. But cats (as well as our cell phone cameras) are equipped with better night vision and can pick them up, because the band of light on their frequency allows this to occur. In short, they have a broader spectrum of vision than we do." All I know is this is absolutely awesome. We are so blessed to live in a time where Spirit seems to be revealing itself to mankind as being very, very real indeed.

In one of Amy's video's you can hear her speaking with an orb she identified as the spirit of her late father. Her father was a very enlightened person who had an awesome understanding of the spirit world himself. He and Amy were very close. His baby picture is on an antique secretarial desk in her living room. In the video Amy speaks to him in a playful manner, the way they used to speak to one another when he was on earth. Amy wrote this note to me, "After I got your message last night, I did a test. It seems as though I can coax them to come out. I've noticed that when I start taping and say something like "Who wants to play?" Or "Is anybody there?" in a friendly voice, they appear almost immediately. If my mood is not at its best, they won't come."

Although rare, energy emitting light orbs revealing themselves under certain conditions are not a new phenomenon. I'd seen similar orbs before in a snapshot taken in 2012 before the start of a mediumship gathering hosted by Theresa Caputo.

The fact that these energy emitting light orbs seem to be showing up more often now may be due to more than just our technological advancements. I'd like to think a large portion of humankind itself is advancing to a level where this type of revelation is happening as a natural precursor into a greater understanding of our partnership with the world of spirit.

In 1984, I took a huge leap of faith to leave a bad relationship and moved to an entirely new city. As I was getting ready for bed one night I had an incredibly strong sensation of being watched. I shook it off, went to bed and fell asleep quickly. All of a sudden I woke up and found myself

139

hovering up near the ceiling of my room! I was acutely aware that my entire body was now much smaller. My entire being existed within an orb-like oval shape. I could see, so I must have had eyes, but I got the distinct impression that I was not much larger than the actual space around my eyes. It felt as if I was looking through a pair of snorkeling goggles. As the dim light from the partially open curtain in my bedroom streamed in from the parking lot outside, I could feel myself floating slowly up and down. I was able to clearly see the sparkly popcorn ceiling, which was right above me. I also remember hearing a low, distinct hum and realized light was coming from within and all around me. I now realize I was exactly like the energy emitting light orbs captured by the camera at Theresa Caputo's mediumship gathering and those orbs which also visit my friends.

While hovering up near the ceiling, I looked around the room and then down at the bed. I saw myself lying there in the same position in which I had fallen asleep just moments before, with my hand positioned up near my left cheek. As soon as I realized that I was detached from my body, a huge rush of fear shot through me. In that exact same moment, I immediately popped back into my body. Now with eyes wide open. This incident lead me to conclude that fear must not be something that exists in the non-physical environment. In that moment, I realized that my SST had been right there with me in this experience and would not allow me to feel fear of any type. It was they who had whooshed me back into my body, as soon as I began to experience any fear.

Although I didn't see them that night, I believe this incident was witnessed by many in spirit, which explains why earlier I distinctly felt like I had "bumped" into someone when I turned around after setting my alarm clock. The whole episode scared me to the point that I had to seek out professional help just in order to be able to sleep peacefully. Interestingly, I had just started attending weekly lectures held by the late Joshua David Stone. In addition to being a licensed psychologist, he was also an awesome spiritual teacher. This occurrence motivated me to make an appointment with him so I could get to sleep without fear of leaving my body again. I ended up becoming a long-term student of his and credit him with a significant amount of my spiritual growth. I suspect the entire event was orchestrated by my spiritual support team as an impetus for pursuing my spiritual path.

I will never forget that evening. It was then that I experienced FIRST HAND being more than a body. We are sparks of the Divine and our true form is that of energy emitting light. Since I was able to leave my body and still be completely alive, that was proof enough for me of our eternal immortality.

After her initial vision of the energy emitting light orbs, Kate invited me to do a psychic reading for her during which it was revealed that there was a child, a baby boy to be exact, who was waiting to be born to her. Shortly after this, without knowing my prediction, another psychic also told Kate the same exact thing.

Around this time a very interesting thing happened with Kate's light orbs. Instead of just swirling around her as they had been doing for several weeks, they began to come together into a larger, more solid looking form. The orbs were still only visible through the lens of her camera, however, they had now coagulated to form a more dense and quite discernable figure. Because of its S like shape, we began calling that larger orb, Casper.

I knew I had been blessed by being able to witness this incredible phenomenon. Being able to actually see individual light orbs on camera was fascinating. However, their coming together as a group to form a larger being was even more incredible. In watching the video you can see Kate passing her hand through the mass slowly. As I observed the color of the skin on her fingers change when they went into the thick, smoky looking substance, while she described the feeling of tingling energy she was experiencing, I stopped doubting and started thinking. I suddenly realized the orbs coming together were likely forming that child we'd identified who was waiting to be born to her. It makes sense that, just like when sperm fertilizes an egg in a woman's uterus and cells begin to multiply, numerous light beings on the spiritual side begin to come together to participate in forming the personality that will incarnate on earth.

142

Kate's recordings of the energy emitting light orbs coming together to form a larger, more dense one helped me realize that we are each made up of many, many orbs - or beings. Just as Kate's orbs came together to form a larger, more dense being, which started creating the beginnings of a child waiting to be born to her, I believe we too are the result of this sacred gathering of numerous souls.

This explains why there are so many different facets to our personalities. Within myself, as I suspect within you, there live numerous personality aspects. One aspect of mine is fearless and strong, the other quiet and shy, one positive, another somewhat pessimistic, one prone to feeling fearful at times, another bold and brazen, and so forth. I also believe one of these beings, part of the group which comes together to form "us" before our physical birth, is chosen to be the leader. Or perhaps more aptly put, the vessel which contains the others. This one I've named "The Custodian." The Custodian has the honor of being in charge of the care of the other orbs, which have come together to form you. It is the one you know as "I." I, as the custodian of the other orbs, has the important job of managing the care and wellbeing of the rest of the souls that make it up. However, because the entire group incarnates together as one human being, the stage, if you will, is shared. Meaning, different aspects get to act as leader in different situations. One aspect of yourself excels in situations that others may not. It is that being's job to teach the others how to be successful in situations they may not be expert in. They signed up to learn from one another. In the movie "The Shack," Jesus says, "It's all about relationship," which supports this understanding. In my own case, the being that heads up Adriana is incredibly loving and supportive - like an awesome parent. It makes sense that this was the one put in charge for me, since God knew I would need this support in my life.

The bible says, "God created mankind in his own image," (Genesis 1:27). Many faiths embrace the fact that the power we call God is actually composed of several beings. Christianity identifies these as the Father, the Son and the Holy Spirit. Each separate, yet functioning as one larger entity. They function together, supporting one another, on behalf of the whole. Just as God serves as the Grand Custodian of us all, you are custodian to the beings who have come together as you.

I realize this is a lot of information that should be incorporated it into it's own book. However, I want you to at least have a basic understanding of the importance of your role as grand custodian of the energy beings you have been entrusted with. Each aspect of your personality is a bonafide individual. A real person. A being unto him/herself. And your role, is to serve *as* God at any given moment to the system of beings that have lovingly come together to experience this lifetime under you care. As you start to become familiar with this concept, you will begin to grasp its huge implications.

The fact is you have many inner beings who made this trip to earth with you. Just like the infinite mirror phenomenon (google it if you are unfamiliar with the term), the universe itself is reflected within each of us. That means, just as we host a multitude of inner beings, we are also part of a larger being ourselves. That being is part of a group of beings that are part of a larger being, and that being is part of a larger being, until there is only One. This explains why -

1) You are much greater than you think. There is incredible power available to you. You just need to learn how to focus your asking and your perspective regarding this grand system of beings.

2) You have a huge responsibility to shepherd, encourage and manage each aspect of yourself. It's through your allowing them to have healthy self expression that they grow. Self love is a huge and incredibly powerful part of all this.

3) You are part of a larger system of peer type spiritual beings who support and encourage you.

4) Just like you are the custodian of smaller orbs, you (as a larger orb of light) are held by an even larger custodian who is responsible for and appreciative of your contribution to the whole.

5) You and your SST are all members of the same larger Soul. Some call this our Soul Tribe. That is why our SSTs are so loving and supportive of us. They are part

of this peer group. You are all working for the same team and rooting for the same wins.

6) Ultimately, the Divine Custodian of all Souls is part of our SST as well.

7) Once you begin to learn how to work within this system and acknowledge your incredibly important role within it, your life will become magical. Perhaps not perfect, but definitely magical.

Why will your life become magical? Because you are now honoring your place within the system. You are now aware of and honoring the system itself. The system accepts your appreciation and support and returns immense appreciation and support back to you. This system is Divinity in action and you are a significant part of it. You own a leadership role within it. You are a significant link and it could not exist without you.

You are as gods walking the earth. You have the model of the entire universe within you. All the various aspects of you, the light beings within you, are like your children. Just as God works to care for and include you as one of God's cherished aspects, you are responsible for caring for your aspects. Rest in the knowledge that you yourself are a special aspect of the Divine. There is no separation between the power we know as God and yourself. Everything that it consists of is available to you.

So there you have it. Now that you realize your part in this incredibly alive system, you can own all the power necessary to truly enjoy it, not just survive it. Yes, own it! You are a part of it. Develop a close relationship with all the various aspects of your own personality, giving each a voice, not leaving anyone to ever feel abandoned, unsupported or left out. Assist them in expressing themselves and growing in the full and healthy manner they came forth to do, which is the role you volunteered for. And, conversely, own your role as part of the grander matrix of all Life. Hold strong to and enjoy your part as a cherished aspect of the whole.

Always strive and make the most of your human-ness. Remember that we are in form for just a short while. In addition to our larger purpose, we also came forth to experience having a body with all sorts of sensory and tactile gifts. Listen to the sounds of nature, smell the scents of life, dance when you can, enjoy music, feel all your feelings. Love yourself. Love life. Love period. Do not be afraid of new adventures. Take risks. This earth life is a special opportunity to grow into a greater sense of appreciating who you are and what you're capable of.

My father was a very intelligent man. I once asked him what he thought happened to us when we die. Although not a particularly religious person, he immediately said he believed we become part of something larger. Even though I didn't really know what he was talking about at the time, I now realize he was absolutely right. Thanks dad. I know you're not

147

just waiting for me on the other side, but here with me now. And I know you're proud of what I've done with that little newspaper clipping you saved for me so long ago.

Blessings to all who read this. May you walk the earth secure in the knowledge of the grand beings you are. May you freely call upon the Team of Light Beings who surround and support you and be available to support those who have entrusted themselves to your care. You are the Sparks of Creation. With faith, courage and love, know your grandness. Own your power as a sacred Being of God's light and love. Stand in it with a mighty fearlessness every moment of every day.

Epilogue

A few weeks after finishing the final chapter of this book, I was experiencing a challenge coming up with suitable artwork for the cover. I'd considered several options, but none seemed to capture the spirit (if you will) of what I hoped to impart. While laying on the couch one afternoon searching my phone for images for inspiration, I received an impulse from Spirit to turn on my camera. By this time, I had experienced several opportunities to view my own light orbs through my camera lens in several spots throughout my house. Once you've experienced this phenomenon for the first time it can become quite addictive. So, I enthusiastically reached for my phone and pressed record. In joyful anticipation, I looked forward to catching a few floating energy light orbs near my feet in the afternoon twilight that bathed my living room. Shock mixed with elation flooded my entire being as I looked into my screen at what my camera lens was capturing. A golden orb trailing a beautiful tail hovered near my feet. Incredulous, I called my husband from the next room to confirm what I was seeing. He peered into my camera lens and saw the same exact scene. In shock, we both stared at it for several minutes. A screenshot of that video has become the cover of this book. You can see the entire video on my website www.revadriana.com.

Bibliographic References:

1) Sudman, Natalie (2012), "Application of Impossible Things – My Near Death Experience in Iraq" *Ozark Mountain Publishing, Inc. (reprinted with permission)*

2) Grout, Pam (2013), "E² - Nine Do-It-Yourself Energy Experiments that Prove Your Thoughts Create Your Reality" *Hay House, Inc.*